T0271221

CHINA
RECONNECTS
Joining a Deep-rooted Past
to a New World Order

CHINA
RECONNECTS
Joining a Deep-rooted Past
to a New World Order

WANG GUNGWU

World Scientific

NEW JERSEY · LONDON · SINGAPORE · BEIJING · SHANGHAI · HONG KONG · TAIPEI · CHENNAI · TOKYO

Published by

World Scientific Publishing Co. Pte. Ltd.
5 Toh Tuck Link, Singapore 596224
USA office: 27 Warren Street, Suite 401-402, Hackensack, NJ 07601
UK office: 57 Shelton Street, Covent Garden, London WC2H 9HE

Library of Congress Control Number: 2018050995

British Library Cataloguing-in-Publication Data
A catalogue record for this book is available from the British Library.

ISBN 978-981-3278-12-7
ISBN 978-981-120-360-2 (pbk)

For any available supplementary material, please visit
https://www.worldscientific.com/worldscibooks/10.1142/11207#t=suppl

Desk Editor: Lixi Dong

Typeset by Stallion Press
Email: enquiries@stallionpress.com

Printed in Singapore

On the occasion of East Asian Institute's 20th Anniversary,
I dedicate the book to my EAI colleagues and friends.

I thank all of them, past and present,
for 22 years of friendship
and for the learning we shared together.

About the Author

Wang Gungwu is University Professor at the National University of Singapore and Professor Emeritus of the Australian National University. He is Foreign Honorary Member of the History Division of the American Academy of Arts and Science and former President of the Australian Academy of the Humanities. He was vice-chancellor of the University of Hong Kong from 1986 to 1995.

His recent books include *Renewal: The Chinese State and the New Global History* (2013); *The Eurasian Core and Its Edges* (2015); *Nanyang: Essays on Heritage* (2018); and *Home is Not Here* (2018).

Contents

Acknowledgments

This volume reflects my latest efforts to look afresh at China while still learning from my EAI colleagues, past and present. Although some of the chapters have come from talks I have given elsewhere, my colleagues will recognize some of the issues that have interested me, having heard me talk about them in our informal seminars and conferences.

I can identify the following occasions where some of the views were presented:

Ishizaka lectures in Tokyo 2007;
Straits Times Global Forum 2016;
Symposium in Stockholm 2016 on "What is China?";
Lecture given at Tsinghua University 2016;
Talks to Foreign Affairs officers in Singapore 2016;
EAI Conferences on Xi Jinping in 2016 and 2018;
International Conference on "A New World Order" in Taipei 2018;
Lectures given at University of Malaya in 2017; Chinese University of Hong Kong in 2017; Nanyang Technological University in 2018; and University of Hong Kong in 2018.

Studying China:
History in the Contemporary

When the East Asian Institute (EAI) was about to celebrate its 20th anniversary in 2017, my colleagues thought we should all write something for the occasion. I wrote a short piece that I include here to remind us of the celebratory occasion.

I also thought I should be more ambitious and put some thoughts together for a book, something that could be related to my joining the Institute and staying for over 22 years. This turned out to be harder to do than I had expected. I have learnt so much from my colleagues and have had to re-learn so much Chinese history while trying to follow what has been happening to China during the last two decades.

For one thing, my stay at the EAI was like another fresh start for me, my fourth, I think. I started hearing about China from my parents as the place to which we would soon return. I began to learn about its culture through its poetry and literature as well as some classical texts. I actually spent a year studying at university in Nanjing. Although China did not become home, those impressionistic years left a deep imprint on my mind.

I then looked away from China for several years, spending time mainly in Malaya-Malaysia but also in Britain. After studying a variety of subjects, I turned to China as a site for historical study. This did not require that I look at China as the People's Republic or study the Chinese people who were going through another violent and unpredictable revolution. Instead, what I began to do was to immerse myself in something called *Hanxue* 汉学 Sinology. It was more like starting again and could be described as my second chance to learn.

This I continued to do when I was teaching Chinese history at the University of Malaya in Singapore and Kuala Lumpur. It was a time when I was much more involved in Southeast Asian history and especially absorbed in the study of the people of Chinese descent who had been active in the region for centuries. My new research gave me a different perspective on China's past and present, something I had not really appreciated before.

When I went to the Australian National University (ANU) in 1968, it was China's Cultural Revolution and the turmoil it brought to the Chinese state and the lives of the Chinese people that made me feel that I knew too little about contemporary China. I decided to learn what was happening there. Canberra and the university had an excellent collection of books, journals and documents and the open research environment allowed me to probe into the multiple dimensions of the Chinese revolutions of the 20th century. My readings also led me to some of China's recent transformations that had made China almost unrecognizable to an historian. I was at the Australian National University (ANU) for 18 years and spent much of the time reflecting on what I learnt. I found myself mesmerized by the vast amount of materials that I had not been able to read in Singapore and Malaysia. I was reorienting my focus and soon came to realize that I was really experiencing yet another start to my understanding of China.

There were limits to what I could learn. I was far away from where China was changing and was constantly reminded that more changes were around the corner. A turning point came when Mao Zedong died and a surprising coup ended his tumultuous era. That was followed by an extraordinary turnaround in policies that kick-started another China run. My colleagues and I followed these changes with several visits to try to keep up with the new pace of development. Then came the opportunity to move to the University of Hong Kong. This was simply irresistible. I could now try to see China up close: how the country was opening up and adjusting to a global market economy that was essentially capitalist, everything that China had spent three decades condemning. My decade in Hong Kong was also a rich mix of learning what Britain wanted to leave behind and how most Hong Kong people welcomed their return to China. I was privileged to share a front seat with people who had been preparing for years for the city to become China's Special Administrative Region. There were anxious moments concerning the autonomy of the city's legal and financial institutions, but the prospect of being part of China's future development seemed attractive and exciting to most of the people.

From that vantage point, I saw China seeking to relocate itself in a new global framework when the Soviet Union fell and the Cold War ended. What struck me was the underlying awareness among many Chinese leaders that the country's future had to be reconnected somehow with its heritage. They were uncertain as to how the people and the country's institutions could absorb the shock of Mao Zedong's damaging experiments with continuous revolution and how they could face the global system now dominated by a single superpower. There were growing signs that a deeper appreciation of China's history, both the recent and the long past, was re-emerging.

One familiar feature of modernity soon appeared. Chinese leaders were keen to channel the nationalist fervor that was resurfacing. Even when eagerly learning from the developed economies of the West, many young Chinese were keen to look back to the best of Chinese heritage. Some were curious how the Nationalists aroused the high patriotism earlier in the century; others revisited the existential threats that Qing China had not seen in time to save its fate. For them, the more they found continuities with their past, the more they realized that reconnecting to the twists and turns of millennia of history, albeit difficult, was rewarding. If done with rigor, studying and researching China's past could provide the mental and cultural ballast that they needed to confront the future. This development gave me much to think about.

When I left Hong Kong to come to Singapore, I came to join the East Asian Institute (EAI) that was set up by Dr Goh Keng Swee, who was then Singapore's 2nd Deputy Prime Minister and Minister for

Education. What made the Institute especially challenging to me was its location in Singapore. My perspective as an historian of China was once again being changed because my EAI colleagues were working in a *Chinese-majority* state that is multi-cultural, multi-linguistic, multi-religious and insistent that it was *not* Chinese. Working with the Institute and discovering the complex subtleties of explaining China under such circumstances was an extraordinary experience.

I had previously been in three different dispensations when I tried to follow how China and the Chinese dealt with the Great Powers and then how they adjusted to a world with two superpowers. I also tried to understand the efforts of smaller countries that wanted to learn how to be neutral during the Cold War. More recently, there have been issues of how to stay that way when dealing with powers like the United States and the People's Republic of China. At other levels, I had looked to understand Maoist China from afar and then, closer by and turning my head right around, to appreciate the reform agenda of Deng Xiaoping. What Dr Goh's Institute was doing was new to me.

I learnt that he wanted the Institute to explain what China was trying to do, what its immediate and long-term interests were and how it planned to do what was necessary when it had so many different peoples spread over such a vast and unevenly developed territory. That was difficult enough. But he wanted even more, that the Institute write not to praise and defend or to judge and criticize what China was doing. In particular, he did not want the Institute to adopt the value systems and theoretical frameworks used in European, American and other similar research centers, especially those not appropriate for describing Chinese conditions. All this called for a different mindset when reading the wide range of sources available. My colleagues have told me how they had been sorely challenged. I would like to think that the EAI has gone a long way towards achieving that.

What my colleagues examined and described over the years has helped me to re-orientate my own understanding of Chinese history. When Zheng Yongnian became Director, he enabled me to continue interacting with my colleagues so that I could keep up-to-date with what was happening. That way, I was able to regularly review my thinking about the parts of Chinese history that were still relevant to the Chinese today. The changes I experienced have made me even more keenly aware how the present and the hopes for the future affect our perspectives of the past. It should be clear in the chapters of this book that, while I learnt a great deal from reading my colleagues' writings and from our many meetings and discussions, any mistakes and misinterpretations are entirely mine.

For me, there was a further bonus. My wife Margaret and I were surprised when we realized that our stay in Singapore since arriving early in January 1996 was the longest we have stayed in any one country or city. During that time, I was privileged to see the Singapore city-state grow further to become the dynamic center of a region with growing economic and political potential. What a difference this is from the colonial city I knew when I first came here as a student in 1949–1954. More than ever, Singapore is the place to be if one wishes to learn how the Southeast Asian region is changing in response to a China that is reinventing itself as a global economic power.

***

On 24 May 2017, when celebrating the EAI's 20th anniversary, I placed on record my thoughts about what the EAI set out to do, offering a short history of its beginnings, followed by some reflections of the work it has done.

Thank you for coming to this special occasion for the East Asian Institute. We are especially grateful to have Deputy Prime Minister Teo Chee Hean here to help us celebrate our anniversary.

In the context of a celebratory moment, I hope you will appreciate my recounting the Institute's history. I believe the story is one that is worth re-telling. It is one with unexpected, even dramatic, turns that reflect the kind of society that Singapore is, the willingness to learn and the ability to respond to new challenges. These are in my mind the keys to the city-state's success in a rapidly changing world.

The Institute's story began with Dr Goh Keng Swee when he was Minister for Education. Dr Goh was concerned for the ethical values that he believed Singapore should stand for. It led him to establish the Institute of East Asian Philosophies to focus on how values of universal validity in the Confucian past could still provide lessons for us today.

Dr Goh then turned the Institute's attention to China's present. This happened after Singapore established diplomatic relations with China in 1990. After two revolutions, China was determined to modernize and rebuild its civilization afresh. Dr Goh chose to study this phenomenon through developments in its political economy. So the Institute's name was changed to the Institute of East Asian Political Economy. Dr Goh then brought in Professor John Wong from the Economics Department to lead the Institute to study in depth the workings of contemporary China.

By the time I joined the Institute as its Executive Chairman in 1996, it had become clear that the demands of such a study should be carried out in close association with a larger research institution. We were fortunate that the National University of Singapore (NUS) under Vice Chancellor Professor Lim Pin was willing to let us join NUS. In our new home, under the name of East Asian Institute, we recruited scholars who specialized in the study of a China that was fast rising in the world. The country's speed of change required careful attention by those who knew it well. It needed people who were trained to examine the complexities of that vast country, one that was determined to make progress as quickly as possible.

Mr George Yeo, then Minister for Information and the Arts, attended our re-opening as part of NUS, and encouraged us to take a broad view of how China was reinventing itself. I was delighted that John Wong agreed to stay and be the Institute's Research Director. We were fortunate that our current Director Zheng Yongnian had also come to join us. With that, the EAI was able to start with confidence.

I. Our Purpose

We have been learning during the past 20 years how much there is to be done. China continues to astonish us by developing faster and in more sophisticated ways than anyone could have imagined. We have now seen how it mastered the latest skills required in an industrialized society and acquired the necessary technologies to do just about anything that the most developed nations of the West are able to do. And, not least, what also amazes me is the concerted effort to connect its modern transformations with China's historic past. This is not merely a country trying to catch up but also one that is planning for a future in which China will once again be a whole and integrated polity. It expects to be strong and prosperous, capable of renewing its distinctive civilization, thus inducing people to treat it with respect.

The 20 years have been exhilarating ones for us at the EAI. But what makes our Institute very special is that we do not advise on, nor formulate, policies for governments to adopt. Nor are we an academic center that analyzes policies and practices for theoretical and comparative study. Our founder Dr Goh had spelt out our purpose, and with the agreement of all concerned, that has remained the same even after we became part of the university. What we do is use our scholarly skills to understand and explain contemporary developments in China, what its leaders are trying to do, the why and how of what is succeeding and what is not. The goal is to assist the government and people of Singapore to grasp the significance of changes in China and help them see their way to deal with that vast country.

We also expect in this way to enable people to check on the media representations of China that are one-sided for or against whatever China does. Thus we recruited those who can be relied upon to provide accurate and up-to-date information of what is happening. In addition, John Wong and Zheng Yongnian have provided guidance and training for younger scholars to hone their skills in this area.

Our job is not to try to determine policies or comment on policymaking, whether done in Singapore or in China. Where Singapore is concerned, we are also not the people to explain this global city to China. As Dr Goh put it very firmly, we must not compromise our task to explain China as best we can. Where Singapore's position is concerned, that should be left to the many specialists in the government and other institutions who are qualified and responsible.

Singapore, indeed, has many who are entrusted with that task. No one has done more to connect with China than the late Minister Mentor Lee Kuan Yew. We knew well how MM Lee represented Singapore's position with both verve and clarity from the time he first met Chairman Mao Zedong over 40 years ago.

DPM Teo, we are grateful that you are able to be here with us today. We know how much you have done to explain Singapore to Chinese leaders. Your experiences and insights will be very helpful as we try to grasp what else we can do to make China more comprehensible to Singapore.

No institution can thrive without a critical look at what it does. It must be prepared to adapt when conditions change. DPM Teo's presence encourages us and makes us feel that our work has been useful and worthwhile. More than that, he is also providing us with an opportunity to hear about how the EAI might do better. That is indeed welcome on a day when we celebrate being 20 years old.

***

Part One

China Dream

Chapter I

Fall and Rise: A Maritime Perspective

When the Qing dynasty fell in 1912, some Chinese saw it primarily as the return to Han Chinese rule and the end of Manchu dominance: this was just and therefore a return to normal. To many others, the fall marked the end of the Emperor-state system: the republic that replaced it was a totally fresh start. The latter was something exciting and challenging and the young in particular responded with revolutionary zeal. But there were yet others who were less confident of the ramifications of something that seemed like a leap into the dark; the uncertainties conjured by the unfamiliar institutions of a republic made them pause. It even created the fear that this could be the end of a civilization that had been so dependent on the centralized Confucian state. In that framework, there loomed the shadow of the Mandate of Heaven *tianming* 天命 and the institutional baggage that conferred legitimacy to the very idea of China. Even the call for revolution *geming* 革命 carried an ambiguous message. It could represent total change to something else altogether or it could promise a better ruling system to replace the one that failed. In that context, without some sense of a mandate, China could end up succumbing to another civilization.

My reading of 20th century Chinese history suggests that these various views and contradictory visions, encouraged further by different sets of models introduced from outside, caused severe tensions within China among its diverse population spread over a huge territory. The feeling of release from a corrupt and deadening *ancien* regime had stimulated different latent aspirations. Some were quick to respond to the most radical ideas while others studied whatever was on offer and were weighing what to import or not. Yet others, perhaps the majority in the countryside, built up an explosive anger, ready to break out of their traditional cages. All that time, foreign powers sought to gain advantage on Chinese soil one way or another adding fire to a flammable state of discontent. The most devastating response was Mao Zedong slogans like "bombard the command center", reject both American capitalism and Soviet socialism, and overthrow just about everything associated with the feudal past. After all that, many would ask, what else was left?

I shall say more in later chapters about the bundle of mixed reactions that plagued China for most of the 20th century with some still lingering in many corners of China today. Here let me concentrate on the idea that China would not fall altogether but could rise again in another shape and manifestation. This was an act of faith that drew on images of displacement, restoration and revival. It called attention to China's own history and encouraged those who knew their history to have reason for hope. In particular, it posed two questions: whether the old system established by the Qin unification could, after 2,000 years, be replaced by something modern and progressive, or whether that centralized state foundation that had enabled China to rise again after falling several times could supply the structure to rebuild the country yet again.

Different groups of revolutionaries and their enemies sought to find the answer to the first question. The second was left for those who, when they thought there was nowhere else to turn to, re-read the country's heritage of texts and records. They saw that China survived and even grew in confidence because various leaders did not only change dynastic houses but had also strengthened the institutions that they inherited each time China was reunified. And the leaders did not have to be Han Chinese; what mattered was that they ruled over Han Chinese more or less the way to which they were accustomed. What was vital was that reunification after a destructive period of division allowed the Chinese to believe that the country was rising again after the fall. And that was celebrated in a huge set of records. I sense that the Chinese Communist Party (CCP) leaders after decades of turmoil and looking at the fruits of successful reforms are revisiting the country's heritage. If they focused on China's ability to rise again after what were total disasters like being conquered by the Mongol and later the Manchu, they could have a surer perspective of the future.

I have suggested in an essay I wrote some years ago that China had fallen three times after the Qin unification. It rose again under the Tang after centuries of fragmentation when the Han fell. When the Tang state disintegrated and could not be restored under the Song, China was overwhelmed by the brute force of Mongol order. The Ming founder then led the third rise and, unexpectedly, China became stronger and even more extended under its Manchu conquerors. Now, after 150 years of their country's decline and precipitous fall, the Chinese are looking to a fourth rise.

I. Nation in Empires

Chinese leaders in 1912 knew that the fall of the dynastic state itself was a much more serious break with the past that anything the country had experienced before. A powerful system was overthrown and its Confucian moral foundations discredited. The Legalist base on which the emperor-state had been built had to be replaced. The loyal Confucians were people whose services were no longer needed. What the new leaders hoped for was that their revolution would enable them to build a modern state modelled on those of the West. They observed what the Japanese had done and had gone further, doing away with the monarchy altogether. In its place would be a constitutional government of elected representatives from all the provinces and the new principles of governance would draw on the methods used by the national empires that defeated China again and again.

As we now know, one revolution was not enough. The nationalist revolution survived the Japanese invasion only to lose in 1949 to a second batch of revolutionaries who were backed by the Soviet Union. This could be said to have been the beginning of China's fourth rise. Unfortunately, Mao Zedong's impatience and the extreme methods he used almost destroyed what the CCP had won. It was not until Deng Xiaoping returned that the fourth rise could begin again.

China has done remarkably well in the last few decades, surprising even people who have studied China for most of their lives. I am as astonished as everyone else at how rapidly the Chinese economy has grown. That is a highly complex story that covers a wide spectrum of issues. I shall only take a maritime perspective here to show how China's rise from a drastic fall this time is different. The steps taken to rise again show that the Chinese are learning to reconnect with their past in innovative ways.

Looking at the fall and rise since the 19th century, I shall pay special attention to the part the Great Powers played in that process and the role of Southeast Asia in the story. The region provided the British and French empires with the bases that were used to open up the China trade to maximize their interests. From there, they forced the Chinese to surrender their coastal assets and created the conditions for China's dramatic fall. But, a century later, it was Southeast Asia that offered opportunities to enable China to rise again.

We often take terms like empire and nation for granted, treating empire as a thing of the past we hope never to see again and assuming that the nation-state is an ideal unit of political organizations. This is misleading. In fact, empires have taken many forms and can never be ruled out while nation-states are new and quite untried in this part of the world. It was only after the 18th century that such states were accepted even in Europe as the best way to organize modern political entities.

As for empire, the word goes back to the Roman *imperium*. When the British and French used it, they were always conscious of its Latin origins. Thus the Roman Empire was the model for modern empires and it has often taken for granted that there has always been something like the Roman Empire down to modern times. For example, the term was loosely applied in Asia to large kingdoms that had expanded their domains. Thus those established by the Chinese, the Mongol and the Mughal had been compared to the Roman Empire. In Southeast Asia, polities like Sriwijaya, Majapahit and Malacca were also called empires.

In fact, while those on the continent had some similar imperial characteristics, those of the archipelago did not have any. Certainly none had histories in any way comparable to that of the Roman republican empire that evolved to become the Christian Holy Roman Empire.

The Chinese empire's relations with its neighbors in the south were based largely on trade and religious affiliations. The respective monarchs nurtured various kinds of feudal and personal ties. Relative power was calibrated to determine whether one should show extra respect, little respect, or no respect at all for one another. These feudal states fought and changed their borders from time to time; what was accepted was a hierarchy of kingly states that could be regulated by varieties of tributary relationships.

After Western European power was extended from the Atlantic to the Pacific and the Indian Oceans in the 16th century, different kinds of empires began to appear. Those in the Americas were colonial empires while those in Asia were primarily empires created to protect trading advantages. The Portuguese who dominated the waters between the Red Sea and the Maluku islands and the Dutch in the Malay Archipelago were not at all like the imperial Romans. They were not territorial but maritime and primarily commercial. They sought to monopolize trade by controlling ports and all trading activities and facilities in the pursuit of profit. The Spanish control of the Philippines resembled their colonial territories in Latin America with an emphasis on Catholic conversion. However, the Philippines' great distance from Spain led its governors to concentrate on commercial interests in China and Japan in ways not different from those of the Portuguese and the Dutch.

Behind this European trade was missionary enterprise. Catholic and Protestant churches did attempt to convert people wherever they could. But what made them rich and powerful were the trading networks backed by advanced shipping technology, the heavily armed warships that sailed freely around the world. That was the beginning of modern globalization.

This maritime global was more genuinely global than the Alexandrian, Mongol and other large empires confined to the Afro-Eurasian landmass. The navies redefined the global while the new empires that they supported enriched Western Europe. Eventually, the British launched the Industrial Revolution that further increased their capacity to control the world.

The new wealth of the Netherlands, Britain and France led to the social and political revolutions that produced the national empires of the 19th century. That process had begun with the Peace of Westphalia in 1648, when treaties signed by a group of Christian states introduced the concept of sovereignty. The states thereby evolved to belong to those living within their borders, citizens who had a common religion and language and shared the same history.

The states created the national empires that became more powerful than the Spanish Empire in Latin America that was the realm of its Royal House. The merchants of London and Amsterdam through their East India Companies laid stronger foundations for their empires. The Dutch revolt that led to independence established the first nation-state. The British nation grew stronger after facing Napoleonic France, the post-revolution product of its *citoyens*. Across the Atlantic, the British there had rebelled against their king and established the United States; theirs became a federation formed out of thirteen colonies, a very distinctive kind of nation-state consisting of colonists and immigrants.

These national empires developed a legal system that was formed to guide the conduct of interstate affairs among European and Christian kingdoms and nation-states. Feudal empires, some headed by "oriental potentates", were not normally included among the civilized entities covered by the law, although the system eventually admitted the feudal Ottoman Turkic and Tsarist Russian empires, and later the Mughal and the Chinese empires. Early texts of international law showed that care was taken to determine whether some countries could be deemed as civilized and worthy of inclusion in the international system. The law obviously did not apply to Southeast Asia polities once they became parts of European national empires.

II. Imperialist Law

When national empires became Great Powers in the scramble for colonies, there developed the ideology that defined the age of imperialism.

That ideology justified whatever the Powers had to do when they collected as many territories as they could. Where China was concerned, the Qing dynasty declined rapidly after the naval powers had successfully used their bases in Southeast Asia to challenge its tributary trading system. Following the British naval victories on the China coasts, China's fall was inevitable.

By that time, large parts of Asia were European colonies or protectorates. The local oligarchies did not know what they could do until they realized that the modern nation was the foundation of European success. None knew how to build a nation but one country responded brilliantly to the challenge. That was Japan. Its leaders saw how the Opium Wars destroyed Chinese defences, how maritime defeats allowed foreign forces to take Hong Kong, control Shanghai and other Treaty Ports and finally open the gates of Beijing. There was immediate danger that Japan would also be similarly overpowered.

They studied China's failures and identified two features that they considered essential if they were to survive. One was that the national empires were based on naval power. The other was that Western international law had finally demolished the Chinese tributary rights long in disuse. The most powerful navy in the world was that of the British, followed by that of the French. As an island country, Japan was sensitive to maritime affairs and they set out to acquire their own naval power by sending their best young people to England to study.

They also learned something that few others in Asia yet understood: it was the nation-state that built these national empires. Japan was more homogenous than any other country in Asia and embarked on building such a state with determination. They replaced the Tokugawa Shogunate with the new Japanese nation under the Emperor Meiji and quickly turned to other European models — Britain for its navy and Bismarck's Germany for its army. They saw how capitalism had enabled the Great Powers to control the global markets and natural resources.

The Japanese were systematic in learning from the West. Perhaps the most brilliant was the way they learnt to use international law to assist them in their expansion. They had lived under the shadow of the formalistic Chinese tribute system and, although the system was not aggressive, it assumed a superior imperial position that the Japanese resented and never accepted. Fortunately, because theirs was an island-state and China was continental-minded, Japan had stayed out of China's reach.

The Japanese always maintained that they were equal to China, though they did not have the power to challenge it. When they saw how this ancient Chinese system was sidelined by international law, they were impressed. Thus when Henry Wheaton's *Elements of International Law* was translated into Chinese, they studied it with great care. When they learnt that the system could determine whether a country was sovereign or not, they used it to claim that the Ryukyu (Okinawa) kingdom was part of Japan. They knew that the Chinese saw it as a tributary, but Ryukyu also paid tribute to the Japanese.

In 1874, the Japanese challenged the Chinese claim. When the aboriginal Paiwan people in Taiwan killed 54 Ryukyu sailors shipwrecked on the island's east coast, Japan sought compensation from Qing China and asked that the aborigines be punished. The Qing government insisted that the sailors were from Ryukyu and not Japan and refused to punish the Taiwanese aborigines on the grounds that they were not Chinese. This left the Japanese free to send troops to attack and kill many of the Paiwan aborigines responsible. Out of the negotiations that followed, the Japanese incorporated Ryukyu as a prefecture of Japan. And, using international law, they questioned China's rights in Taiwan. This paved the way for Japan to add Taiwan to the Japanese empire when they defeated Qing China in 1894.

This story illustrates the first use of the international legal system by an Asian power against an Asian power that did not grasp the significance of that system. Taiwan had been a prefecture of Fujian province since 1684 and was made a separate province in 1887. However, since China admitted that it was not responsible for the actions of the aborigines, its sovereignty over the island was left open. The experience did teach the Chinese how the system had undermined the one that they had maintained, but their officials were slow to respond when the law was brought to bear on it.

Japan also saw what the West had done to lands like Vietnam and Burma that China had treated as tributaries. It now saw an opportunity to make its own move on the Korean peninsula. The Korean king paid tribute to the Chinese emperor but that did not make it any part of China. Therefore, in line with international law, Japan insisted that Korea be treated as sovereign. The Koreans were persuaded to sign trade treaties with the British and the Japanese. With the treaties signed, it was no longer China's responsibility. This paved the way for Japan to move into Korea a few years later. The lesson China eventually learnt was that it must be careful with laws that it had no part in making, especially when these were clearly against China's interests. Chinese leaders must always ask that such laws be reconsidered.

III. Turning to the Sea

The precipitous fall of China can be traced to the lack of naval power and the failure to understand that, in international law, Qing China was the Manchu empire. It was, therefore, comparable to feudal empires like the Ottoman, Austro-Hungarian and Mughal empires that could be dismembered to become several nation-states. Qing China's failure to recognize how the world had changed cost the court dearly. The Han Chinese entrepreneurs found that most foreign capitalist enterprises in Chinese ports were doing what British and the French trading companies and agency houses could do in their colonies in India and Indo-China. Manchu Qing was little better than a semi-colony.

Thus in the eyes of men like Sun Yat-sen and other southern Han Chinese, Manchu rule was not only illegitimate but also helpless. His weak coalition of rebels discovered how useless the Qing had become when they and their allies were able to force it to give way to the Republic of China without much fanfare. The acceptance of a republic modelled on France and the United States was unexpected and extraordinary because, for most Chinese, what this meant was hardly understood. What the rebels agreed on was to end the dynastic system with a presidential system. The confused conditions after 1912 simply encouraged several military commanders to fight among themselves for the next 20 years. This warlordism divided the country so badly that China grew weaker every year.

Some economists have calculated that by 1800 when the Qing dynasty was at the height of its power, China had something like a third of the world's wealth. That may be exaggerated, but not by much. By the end of the century, it was down to under 10 percent. By the second decade of the 20th century, the economy had fallen even further. The Kuomintang party led by Sun Yat-sen was forced to reorganize in order to survive. When Lenin and the Communist International sent agents to offer advice, the party agreed to invite supporters of the newly formed Chinese Communist Party (CCP) to join the party. With Soviet military help, the nationalists eventually defeated the leading warlords, but that simply led to an even more bitter civil war fought between the former partners.

During that entire period, the Japanese were expanding their national empire. The concept of nation was gaining acceptance and Asian leaders everywhere watched Japan build its empire with admiration. Nobody was much concerned as to what this might mean for the future though it was obvious that the Japanese by 1930 had a large empire that included parts of the Asian mainland. After Korea and Manchuria, the Japanese dominated Shandong province, moved into Inner Mongolia and North China, and were pushing towards areas close to Beiping (Beijing). Their economic influence was also spreading into the rest of China.

It was at that point that Chiang Kai-shek's Nationalist government decided to fight Japan. The Nationalists had not been able to unite China and had been fighting a civil war for 10 years. The country was divided among at least three major groups: the Kuomintang loyalists, the CCP with their supporters amongst the peasantry, and the remnants of warlords in different parts of China. While there were many calls for national unity, the three groups were unable to cooperate effectively against the common enemy.

The war in 1937 lasted eight years during which the Japanese military was clearly superior. In addition to ruling over Korea and Taiwan and controlling Manchukuo through a puppet regime, they also had eastern parts of China run by Chinese leaders loyal to or dependent on them. Nationalist leaders like Wang Jingwei joined the Japanese and set up the puppet government in Nanjing. The Japanese had been active among the Mongols and focused on those in Inner Mongolia after Soviet Russia had made Outer Mongolia into its satellite state. The dismemberment of China was almost half-done.

China was saved only because the Japanese brought the United States into the war. President Roosevelt thought that the Japanese were wrong to invade China and did not want the Japanese national empire to take all of it. He was suspicious of imperialism and thought the time had come for national empires to be wound up. Japan's attack on Pearl Harbor in 1941 provided the excuse for him to bring the Americans into World War II. While they did not fight to save China, they appreciated that the Chinese were tying down large numbers of Japanese troops on the continent. This made it easier for the Americans to concentrate on fighting the Japanese at sea. With the world's most powerful navy, the Americans were able to defeat Japan in the Pacific.

Thus China survived the eight-year war. The Nationalist government returned to its capital in Nanjing but could not control much of the rural interior. Nevertheless, Chiang Kai-shek launched a civil war against the Communists. I was in Nanjing studying at university and was really surprised to learn how weak the government forces were. The communists moved quickly into Manchuria where the Russians helped to arm them. By the end of 1948, the People's Liberation Army (PLA) had taken much of North China and, a few months later, the regime changed hands. It is important to remember that the PLA did not have any ships and won entirely on the battlefield.

History in China since 1949 saw a Mao Zedong period and the years after his death. Here I shall only mention that Mao Zedong moved considerable strategic resources further inland to Western China in order to fulfil his revolutionary ambitions. However, under Deng Xiaoping's reforms, that was reversed and China turned around to look out to sea.

I shall not dwell on the first period here. After the nightmare of the Cultural Revolution, Deng Xiaoping opened up the country. The history of the 30 years after 1978 has not yet been fully told, and I cannot say that I understand everything about that period. What I can say is that it was a major corrective to what Mao Zedong had done. Deng Xiaoping saw the sea as the gateway for economic development. During his 15 years in charge, more ports were opened to the global market economy. While carefully avoiding the use of the word capitalism, he advocated the use of capitalist methods wherever he thought appropriate. By opening China up to foreign investment and industrial modernization, he continued to rebuild the centralized state to ensure that the final goal remains that of achieving his socialist ideals.

China followed the trajectory of capitalist growth, notably that of Japan and the Four Asian Tigers (Hong Kong, Singapore, South Korea and Taiwan) and used the sea to transport its manufacturing goods and import the raw materials it needed. Now the region is learning what it is like when China is risen once again. I mentioned earlier the two aspects that had hastened China's fall a century earlier. Interestingly, they are more relevant than ever. The first concerns naval power and the second the politics of international law. On both those, Chinese leaders had made mistakes. Their remedial moves ever since may be summed up as, build a credible navy and take advantage of the laws and institutions that support the international system.

During the Cold War, Mao Zedong depended on continental Soviet power and focused on ideological issues in international affairs. This hampered China's economic development. In contrast, Deng Xiaoping sent some of his ablest cadres to study how the United Nations worked and master the best diplomatic practices when dealing with the outside world. In that way, he worked hard to enhance China's image abroad by adhering to international rules and organizations.

Building a credible navy, however, was a different story. That required large economic resources. It was not until the economy had expanded before the Chinese could start to build such a navy. That did not begin in earnest until the 1990s. Symbolically, it was marked by China buying a second-hand aircraft carrier from Ukraine. Many found that laughable at the time. The Soviet-built carrier was left with Ukraine and the Ukrainians sold it to the Chinese. The Chinese used it to learn how such carriers were built and how they could be used.

It is an over-simplification, but it can be said that China began to look seriously at ways to project naval power beyond their coasts.

China had long known that it needed a modern navy but never had the resources to develop one. When the PLA won against the Nationalists, they did not have a single ship. I was fascinated when I learnt that the PLA generals started thinking about having a navy only when they had to cross the Yangtze River to take Nanjing and Shanghai. When they tried to build their own navy, they only had their Russian allies to help them. The Russians never had much of a naval tradition, so the Chinese really had to struggle even to get started.

We now see the rise of a new navy. The Chinese know they have a long way to go to match that of the Americans. When the Western media talk about how this navy is seeking to threaten or conquer the world, it is simply alarmist exaggeration. The Chinese navy will not be able to do that with the US navy parked outside China's front doors. What the Chinese can do, however, is to deter foreign navies from getting too close to their coasts. They have built submarines and destroyers and have the intercontinental missiles to protect them from naval attacks. But what they really want is to be credible as a maritime nation, one that can also help defend the market economy on which they now heavily depend.

IV. ASEAN

This brings me back to Southeast Asia. Most people do not realize how important the region is to China, especially after the region's decolonization and the establishment of its nation-states. Were it not for that, the imperial powers would still be there. But decolonization has meant that no foreign powers now dominate the region and the Chinese certainly hope that will remain so.

Decolonization removed the various naval threats from the China coast and pushed them further out. And, with the end of the Cold War, China has been able to start afresh to deal with the new nations. China does not yet know how to do that well because this is a new strategic environment. It is nothing like the old tributary system and there is no way the region would want that to return. The states are now operating in an international system that seeks to function through adherence to international law. And, since the 1990s, the 10 nations in Southeast Asia have been working hard to develop a community of shared interests. China knows that it has to learn to deal sensitively with this Association of Southeast Asian Nations (ASEAN).

At the same time, something else has happened that few anticipated. I refer to the rise of China's economy together with that of India. Few people expected that to happen so quickly. And, with the economic power of Japan still strong, Asia is moving towards a new stage in historical development. There are signs that the center of economic dynamism will move from the North Atlantic to the Indo-Pacific. Here I use the historical Indo-(Western) Pacific and not Asia-Pacific not only because of the larger region's commitment to the global market economy but also to remind us that peaceful trade had characterized interstate relations for millennia. That was the norm for a flourishing trade with the old China. Now that the Chinese understand the importance of the maritime economy, they know that their future economic development will depend on keeping the seas open. In that context, Southeast Asia's place becomes very different indeed. It will be not only a passageway between the two oceans but also central to new strategic readjustments increasingly important for everyone.

I mentioned earlier that China needs the naval credibility to defend their maritime access to resources and markets. Chinese leaders also have to master the legal intricacies of the international system. They do know how the world order operates as a system based on the rule of law and realize that they must also master the best ways to navigate in that terrain. Here the South China Sea is a crucial test. Chinese merchants and fishermen have long known that the sea was vital to their maritime interests. They also know that it is similarly valuable to Vietnam, the Philippines and Malaysia, and also to Cambodia and Thailand. But there had never been agreed demarcations on the map — international law only began to cover the South China Sea in the 1970s.

It was through UNCLOS (United Nations Convention on the Law of the Seas, effective in 1994) that a treaty to sort out the rights and responsibilities of nations concerning the use of the oceans was agreed on. This was a very complicated matter because so many of the issues involved were new. When the Chinese attended UNCLOS meetings in 1973, they were still new to the United Nations, having just joined it in October 1972. They were cautious and were not sure how the new agreement would be applied. They thought their own position was secure from future problems when it was agreed to set aside all questions pertaining to sovereignty claims.

The idea of sovereignty based on the Westphalian Peace in Europe was new to Asia. Even in Europe, its meaning has sometimes been disputed. Today nation-states, and especially the new ones, see sovereignty as something sacred that has always been there. That is not correct. As defined by the treaties of Westphalia, it still had to be revisited and it was only in the 19th century that international law made sovereignty something that could be legally tested. Where Asia was concerned, it was only with the establishment of the United Nations in 1945 and in the context of decolonization that sovereignty became crucial to enable countries to justify their post-colonial borders. There are issues still evolving, for example, how international law should be applied to the sea.

As the debates continue, this is still work in progress. The Chinese have had problems with that. In their own history, they had never thought of permanent sovereign borders and certainly never encountered anything like international law. As shown earlier, they were so innocent that the Japanese were able to interpret international law to their advantage and thereby created problems for the Qing Empire that are still relevant.

I do not fully understand how international law can be implemented with regards to sovereignty claims in the sea. It is a very complex subject that international legal experts still argue about. That does not mean that a solution is not in sight, but it does indicate that there are areas in international law that are not clear-cut. The Chinese have in their tradition a feature that is difficult to explain. It is the assumption that law is totally man-made and can be changed when the people concerned find it a hindrance and no longer useful. When that happens, the protagonists would seek to have the law changed. Nothing about law is sacred.

However, in Western Europe, the tradition is different. The international law first developed among Christian kingdoms and empires was based on principles opposite to those of the Chinese. There was an underlying assumption that legal agreement was answerable to God, hence the touch of the moral and sacred behind the rule of law. The Chinese could not see how the Great Powers were backed by anything sacred or moral when they applied their international law to China and have been sensitive and suspicious ever since.

I shall deal with the question of rule of law in a later chapter. Here I shall merely point out why the Chinese believe that reasonable people can always unmake laws that are no longer helpful and make new ones to meet changing conditions. The difference in understanding has led to difficult relationships that are likely to remain with us for a while yet. There is plenty of room for disagreement in the South China Sea issue. This is unfortunate because it is of crucial importance to the region. That Sea borders on eight of the 10 ASEAN members as well as the southern coast of China and all concerned have to negotiate with sincerity and sensitivity.

This takes us back to the rise of China. This has clearly been unlike the three previous times it rose again after having fallen. This time, the world has radically changed and the fourth rise is closely related to the maritime nature of the global market economy. Also, the world order is now one of equal and sovereign nations. And Southeast Asia has become a regional player with ASEAN as China's strategic neighbor. As long as the world is focused on the Indo-Pacific, Southeast Asia will have a central role. What ASEAN members do is already being closely scrutinized; with the organization in the spotlight, how it builds the trust necessary to enable it always to speak with one voice has never been so vital.

This rising China is deeply interested in cooperating with ASEAN and seems to be planning accordingly. It is a clear example of how aware it is that the world is like nothing in the past. This can also be seen in initiatives like the New Silk Roads that Xi Jinping has proclaimed as a priority project crucial to China's future development. The Belt and Road Initiative certainly can help those involved to reconfigure what it means for the world's economic centre to move to this part of the world. China is conscious that two-thirds of its boundaries are overland and one-third coastal. This ambitious project could therefore enable China to reconnect its commitments on both land and sea. How the Chinese balance their relationships with their continental neighbors across central Asia against those with their maritime neighbors of the Western Pacific and Indian Oceans will be a measure of what China's rise really means.

Chapter II

Behind the Dream

After studying China history for decades, I noticed how some things kept coming up again. The China Dream is one of them. When I was growing up in British Malaya, I was told of Sun Yat-sen's dream, as seen in the name of the society he founded in 1894, the Revive China Society 兴中会. I also recall my father explaining to me that Sun Yat-sen's dream could be traced further back in Chinese history. It had come from the Ming loyalists who had organized secret societies to chase out the Manchu and restore the country to Han Chinese rule. He also thought that Revive China echoed the call by Zhu Yuanzhang, the Ming founder, for Han Chinese to drive out the Mongols in the 14th century.

Since then, I have taken every China dream to have something to do with reviving China. However, reading about Xi Jinping's China Dream these past years, I can see why he sees the revived China playing a role in world affairs that is commensurate with a modern economic power with ancient roots. There is the urge to see China's future as a modern state in an evolving world order, but there is an inclination to link with some of the continuities that had provided China with resilience, wisdom and longevity.

At its core, Xi Jinping's China dream seems to begin with the hopes that most Chinese had shared at Tiananmen on October 1, 1949 when Mao Zedong spoke to the nation. The corrupt regime was overthrown and New China was beckoning on the horizon. I have no clear recollection of how that dream differed from Revive China because, having returned to Malaya in late 1948, I heard no more about the China Dream. Malaya had its own nation-building to do and I joined many of my generation to learn about that. Years later, we read about the Great Leap Forward that brought famines to some of the ablest peasant cultivators in the country and then about the Cultural Revolution that Mao Zedong launched against his senior revolutionary comrades. Perhaps there was a newer Mao Zedong dream in which revolutions never end, but I have never met anyone who believed that such a dream could ever come true.

Living outside China, I regularly met Chinese who still dreamt hopefully for the future of China. Among overseas Chinese whose hometowns were in Southeast Asia, Australia or North America, their dream was usually for a peaceful and prosperous China. In Hong Kong, I did meet some people who had only Maoist nightmares whenever they recalled relatives and friends who escaped to the colony. In 1973, on my first visit to the People's Republic of China, I had the chance to see the Cultural Revolution for myself. I saw a damaged land and met many who were struggling to understand what Mao Zedong really wanted. I came away thinking that this was a revolution that had gone awry. It was many years later that I fully appreciated how much destruction of lives and property had occurred in the 1966–1968 period, compared to which the later half of the Cultural Revolution harmed fewer people. Recalling all this, I am not sure what lessons Xi Jinping really wants his party colleagues to remember from Mao Zedong's thirty years.

Not long after Deng Xiaoping started on his reforms, I was struck by the fact that some people were ready to talk about a China Dream again. The dream pendulum seemed to have swung back a little. This time it was down to earth, or in the words widely used then, feeling for the stones while crossing to the other, presumably brighter, side. People were inspired to work hard and some dreamt of learning as much as possible from the advanced economies of the world. But there was an emphasis on patience and modesty. Theirs were lesser dreams, some woven into hopes to build new lives abroad and not return.

Deng Xiaoping's reforms were extraordinarily life giving. They occurred when the Cold War was turning around and, for the Chinese people, the mood was sober, a time for tireless achievement. The results, as it turned out, were breathtaking. Without talking up hopes and dreams, the Deng Xiaoping era provided China with its most constructive and wealth-making years in at least two centuries. High hopes were raised, not least in Hong Kong. It was there in the late 1980s that I first heard "My China Dream" sung in Putonghua and well-received in the PRC as well the Cantonese song of hope "China Dream". Both songs were written by Huang Zhan 黄沾. The final lines of the second reminded me of Sun Yat-sen's Revive China call.

> "The countless dreams these five thousand years contain the same one thing, they want each and every Chinese to become free and fortunate like me."

That was the other end of the dream spectrum for people who were recovering from want and fear and uncertainty about when wealth and power might return to their country. Today, Chinese leaders have gone beyond Sun Yat-sen's Revive China dream. Their pride in national regeneration meshes with Xi Jinping's focus on achievable global reach and, from the number of new songs written to celebrate his dream, it would appear that most people share it.

Therefore, I was shocked when the CCP removed the term limit on the presidency from their Constitution and proclaimed the advent of Xi Jinping Thought on socialism. It had not occurred to me that he would abandon one of the key political reforms that was made to avoid any sniff of a personality cult. When it was explained that his vision was long-term and that he needed more time to realize his ambitious dream, it seemed reasonable to allow him some flexibility. Nonetheless, I was astonished how readily his party colleagues had agreed to support the move. I do not know if Xi Jinping intends to remain president for life or simply wants the right to continue until he finds a worthy successor, someone who fully shares his dream.

I noted how many commentators and analysts were quick to ask if Xi Jinping was going to be a Mao Zedong. That was not the question I would have asked but if asked, I would say that he will not. Nevertheless, I imagine that, under similar conditions, he could try to be. I do not, however, believe such a comparison is important. He will have to be very different because he has inherited a basket of new problems that Mao Zedong, or for that matter Deng Xiaoping, never had to deal with.

There were other speculations: one that was seriously discussed was that this constitutional change might have benefits in the short-term but would make the longer-term prospects of stable development more uncertain. Here I think the questioners may have missed an aspect of Xi Jinping's approach to China's development as a socialist state: his obvious interest in connecting China's global future to the country's long history. In particular, he seems to be identifying those factors that had strengthened the Chinese state and might help the country withstand the destructive processes of modernization. How can those past experiences be harnessed to help China continue on the road to progress?

I. Learn from the Past

One of the first things that Xi Jinping did when he came to power was to remind his CCP colleagues of the failures of the Soviet Communist Party. He repeatedly called on them to reflect on what the CCP would have to do if it is to survive. Following that, he ended the policy that disconnected Deng Xiaoping's period of reforms from Mao Zedong's three disruptive decades. He wanted Party members to understand what Deng Xiaoping learnt from the Maoist years that led him to change course successfully. In addition, he also asked his colleagues to learn from other mistakes made by many Chinese leaders in the past, not least the nationalists who struggled through the first half of the 20th century.

These exhortations to learn from the past do not make the headlines because they are overshadowed by Xi Jinping's unrelenting campaign against corruption. That has enabled him to remove some of the most senior members of the CCP who had profited from the leadership of his two predecessors. Also, there has been greater attention to the task of economic restructuring. China's export-oriented policy was at a turning point. Naturally, questions about the economy received more attention, especially when official answers were not always convincing.

Xi Jinping has been surprisingly successful in dealing with the People's Liberation Army (PLA). When he spoke of the spirit of winning battles 打胜仗, he was exhorting the armed forces to concentrate on defending the country's growing interests. The PLA should not only focus on becoming professional and updating their military capacity but must also abandon the greed and ambition that had discredited their most senior leaders. His call has inspired younger officers to regain self-respect and has restored their unquestioning faith in the CCP. He then enjoined the PLA to relearn the spirit of revolution and restore the discipline that had enabled it to reunite the country 60 years earlier.

What is striking is that Xi Jinping regularly stresses that the Dream requires everyone to push for progress and modernity while learning lessons from the past. It appears that getting his colleagues to develop a sense of continuity with China's past has become the running theme behind the reforms being advocated. In that context, I think the fears aroused about his policies leading him to become another Mao Zedong are misplaced. Mao Zedong was a very complex leader, having been called, among other things, an iconoclast, a revolutionary, a tyrant and a would-be emperor.

Xi Jinping certainly cannot be the god-emperor that launched the Cultural Revolution and brought China to near disaster. Nor could he be the populist rebel prepared to destroy the Party when he could not get his way. And he cannot be the leader who fought the revolutionary war to found the People's Republic. But could he perhaps be compared to the Mao Zedong who dreamt of China leading a socialist *tianxia* and offering a vision of Sinicized internationalism that was comparable to that of Marx, Engels, Lenin and Stalin? There is nothing to suggest that Xi Jinping would be interested in such adventurism.

However, there was the younger Mao Zedong who might still be an inspiration. This was the man who tamed a fractious party at a time of crisis following the defeat of the Jiangxi soviet and emerged as its leader during the Long March. He consolidated control of the restructured party in Yan'an and led the CCP to fight guerrilla wars against the Japanese. By 1942, he had forged a strong centrist system with him fully in charge. He showed immense cunning and was determined to acquire power within the party at all costs. He developed techniques for manipulating his comrades and destroying those who were slow to obey. At the same time, he was also able to inspire heroic actions from his dedicated cadres. Perhaps Xi Jinping could see himself learning from that in order to bring the party under control.

Mao Zedong also believed in a unified China and his reading of Chinese history persuaded him that he was a worthy successor of the great founding emperors. At the same time, his admiration of Marx and Lenin led him to develop an idiosyncratic worldview. Xi Jinping, on the other hand, seems to be offering goals that are more down-to-earth, for example, the One Belt One Road Initiative that is envisioned to link the Afro-Eurasian landmass by sea and land. What he hopes developing countries can learn from China also seems modest. As far as China's position in the world order is concerned, he has been realistic and does not have any illusions about replacing the United States as the global power.

He has learnt a great deal from the example of Deng Xiaoping, someone who thought deeply about what he could do for his country and was always willing to be adaptable. Deng Xiaoping earned his leadership position by surviving years of treachery and irrationality among his party colleagues. When he finally attained power, he set out to reverse most of the policies that Mao Zedong had launched. He was a practical man who took over leadership when that was necessary, but he was not an opportunist. To the end, he remained loyal to the ideals that led him to join the Party when he was a worker-student in France.

Xi Jinping did not have to endure such trying challenges and does not have to reverse Deng Xiaoping's reform policies. He can still learn from Deng's openness and willingness to change. So far, he has been innovative in the methods he used to bring the Party organization to heel. Like Deng Xiaoping, he has been willing to experiment with new ideas when older ones were no longer working. He has adopted a similar vision for people's wellbeing, but has gone further than Deng Xiaoping in prioritizing stability and order in the quest for a stronger national cohesion.

Xi Jinping has also been explicit about looking to Karl Marx for inspiration, especially going beyond capitalism after building strong economic foundations. Like Deng Xiaoping, he kept his faith in socialism and is no less convinced that this socialism would have Chinese characteristics, drawing on the enduring cultural values that most educated Chinese believe had made the Chinese civilization great. Significantly, at the core of these values is the belief that China needs strong and responsible leaders who are able to bring order and prosperity to people's lives.

II. The Generation after the Reforms

Xi Jinping belongs to the generation that benefitted from Deng Xiaoping's vision and has made a commitment to go beyond what has been achieved so far. He now faces a different kind of crisis. The party that had been saved to become one of the most successful communist parties anywhere has become corrupted beyond recognition. He has been trying since he took over in 2012 from Hu Jintao to amass enough power to do what he thinks is vital for China's future; and that is to save the CCP and thus save the country.

His career from Hebei to Fujian, Zhejiang to Shanghai allowed him to see how the Party swelled with ambitious members. He watched the growing corruption in their ranks that has now reached danger point. In particular, he saw how helpless Hu Jintao and Wen Jiabao were when they identified some serious problems but could do nothing to correct them. He also saw his contemporary Bo Xilai ruthlessly punishing incompetents and decadents in the CCP while himself being arbitrary and corrupt. Ironically, it was a badly fragmented party leadership that enabled Xi Jinping to emerge as Secretary-General. He must have wondered how a recently reformed socialist country could be so quickly overcome by self-interest and greed.

Xi Jinping also saw how the collective leadership that was introduced had become ineffectual by being headless and paralyzed by inaction. His struggles against corruption in high places have been very difficult and he is known to have made many enemies. Furthermore, without strong legal and judicial processes that are transparent and widely respected, there are also questions being asked as to whether justice has always been done. His successes so far have earned him popular support. But the Party's troubles are more pervasive, and anti-corruption measures have also led to suspicion, anxiety and inaction within the government.

He seems to be aware that the economy needs to be restructured and is trying to make the necessary corrections while adhering to a policy of engagement with global markets. But there are growing tensions within the party about how to correct the country's over-dependence on state-owned enterprises and industrial exports. He knows that painful actions have to be taken and expects the Party's cadres to do so efficiently. He does not believe that the private sector can be of much help here. Instead, he is counting on a disciplined Party to regain the faith of the people. This may not be enough but he seems to have focused on this as the only solution he can find.

The party-state had a limited term for its leader. It expected the power centres to select his successor from within a group of potential leaders. Xi Jinping knows that what he aims to achieve cannot be done during his two terms. Even Deng Xiaoping, with all his extraordinary authority, needed 20 more years to keep his reforms on course and chose two successors, Jiang Zemin and Hu Jintao, to make sure that the development momentum was maintained. The two successors each had two terms, thus the 20 years of continuity. Now Xi Jinping seems determined to provide the country with a similar degree of certainty. Removing the term-limits would give him more time to achieve his China Dream.

He has done well to bring the PLA on side and has exhorted its officers not only to be professional and modern but also loyal. He is making deep changes to the Party and its youth wing and has consistently exhorted their members to re-dedicate themselves to the discipline needed for them to become credible again. These and other reforms will need more than two 5-year terms to achieve. To ensure that what he has initiated would be carried through, Xi Jinping has become the Party's new core *hexin* 核心. That would give him the right to choose his successors personally. If he can do what Deng Xiaoping did and find the right leaders to succeed him, he would not have to be upfront in his old age but could sit back and watch his plans being carried out.

Like Deng Xiaoping, he speaks of Chinese characteristics at the heart of his socialism. He has asked that the future China should embody what had been successful in China's past. He may see his job as helping to graft that spirit onto the kind of socialism that China will produce. To do that, he would have to learn from the successes and failures of both Deng Xiaoping and Mao Zedong. In addition, he seems willing to acknowledge the contributions of earlier revolutionary leaders like Sun Yat-sen and, not least, the scientists and engineers who enabled China to be a modern industrial and technologically savvy nation. It is less clear how much he respects the Confucian literati who, at their best, enabled the Chinese state to be successful for millennia. But he does seem aware that the literati compiled the records that were central to the state's legitimacy and these records also provided the framework by which the ideals embedded in the Confucian classical texts could be continuously refined and reinterpreted.

Where the outside world is concerned, events have not been under China's control for over a century. It is only recently that the Chinese have learnt to respond fast to unexpected changes in world affairs. Mao Zedong in his time wanted to influence global events by active involvement in the Cold War. That turned out to be illusory and even counterproductive. Deng Xiaoping, however, knew that nothing could be achieved without the economic development that fully supports the country's defence and security capacities. He was patient and took a "watch and see" attitude. Twenty years after his death, there are now global forces at work that no one could have anticipated. For example, there has been American military activism and overreach in the Middle East and Eastern Europe after the end of the Cold War. Then there is the populist reaction against the social and economic consequences of globalism that has produced growing uncertainty in world affairs.

These forces have led to major changes in the Indo-Pacific region. Xi Jinping now believes that China has the capacity to play a larger role and should be more active in guarding its interests. He wants China to deal with uncertainties and anticipate further changes and must be assured of stability within the country. Chinese history has taught that China should always fear the state of *neiyou waihuan* 内忧外患, internal troubles accompanied by outside threats.

As for the faith in strong leadership, Xi Jinping has taken steps to build his team to deal with a better-educated citizenry. China is now a dynamic society with higher expectations of the Party and its leader. Xi Jinping would want to erect a platform on which his best people would share his Dream. A good example of the dream in action is the Asian Infrastructure Investment Bank accompanied by the One Belt One Road initiative (also known as the Belt and Road Initiative or BRI) that seem to be parts of a grand strategy.

Most Chinese people since the first revolution have looked out for powerful rulers. Although Sun Yat-sen wanted China to become democratic, his party needed a strong leader with supreme power. Following the victory of the Russian revolution, he turned to Soviet advisers to build a revolutionary army and took the first step to establish a party-state 党国 *dangguo*. For Xi Jinping, the lesson was not that nationalism failed but that Sun Yat-sen did not have a strong successor to carry out his plans. The party was divided into rival groups that could not unite even when faced with Japanese invasion. The military leader Chiang Kai-shek who took control simply did not have the political skill and vision to inspire his party colleagues.

Xi Jinping acknowledges that China has had important connections with world history. The country imported nationalism to establish the Republic, Soviet socialism to inspire the PRC, as well as the capitalist methods that Deng Xiaoping chose to enrich the country, and much more that arrived with them. Together with China's own heritage, they contributed to the country's recovery and made the Chinese revolutionary experience different from any other. In that context, Xi Jinping's success in gathering power so quickly is astonishing. He must be aware that such fast gains can plant the seeds of equally swift losses. Thus he probably needs greater care to fulfil his plans for progress: they would have to be consolidated at each stage. Indeed, he has outlined some of his goals for the next 10, 20 or even 30 years.

These goals have to be attained at a time when the world is changing at a rate faster than ever with many unpredictable consequences. Having painted such a future, Xi Jinping cannot pretend that all will follow smoothly. Nor can his colleagues be certain that they could choose as his successor someone with the same sense of direction and purpose. This may be why Xi Jinping did not find it difficult to persuade them to accept the constitutional changes that allow him to be the strongman who could lead the party to save China.

III. An Alternative Path

The CCP believes that centralized power is necessary because the country faces structural problems within and uncertainties abroad. It may not be a coincidence that the return to authoritarian rule has come together with the decline of the liberal consensus in the US and Western Europe. After the democratic advances for several decades, people are less confident today of the efficacy of liberalism. The urge to return to protectionism has grown. In addition, the potential shift in economic dynamism away from the north Atlantic and the election of a US president determined to abandon his country's liberal heritage have heightened the sense of uncertainty. Thus when China under Xi Jinping is offering an illiberal alternative, alarm bells are ringing about those developing states that find liberal democracy irksome and who would welcome a China model.

Xi Jinping has not claimed that China is an alternative to the liberal model. But he is confident about what kind of modernity China needs, and what areas of science, technology and economic diversification should have high priority. He has also made clear which parts of the liberal package China can do without. This leads him to ask his people to look to their past for inspiration, albeit selectively. The wish to do so is nothing new but his calls to identify continuities with China's past have a more focused trajectory.

China had previously learnt from the West when "Western Heaven" 西天 conjured up wondrous images of truth and beauty and included ideas, institutions and artifacts that enriched Chinese civilization. Buddhism from India, Central and Southeast Asia, in particular, embodied great wisdom. So much so that scholars in the Song dynasty came to believe that they had taken enough from the outside to reach the greatest heights and it was unnecessary to take other alien ideas and institutions seriously thereafter. Hence their indifference to the Europeans who arrived after the 16th century. The only exceptions were Matteo Ricci and his band of Jesuits who had found much in China to admire. Some mandarins were impressed by the civilization produced in Renaissance Europe. Today many Chinese regret that they did not pursue that new knowledge more assiduously.

European merchants saw a different China. Behind their elegant robes, Ming and Qing mandarins were to them no less greedy and inefficient than officials elsewhere. They concluded that the Chinese were backward and deserved to be treated accordingly. Thus in the 19th century, they saw themselves bringing superior ideas of law and civility. Christian missionaries were allowed to follow them to save the souls of China's superstitious people. It did not take long for the image of a great civilization to be dismissed. By the end of the century, the West saw a country with a decaying set of institutions that needed only a small push to collapse on its own weight.

How could this deep-rooted system be undone so quickly? The speed of its demise drove many Chinese to reject their past. Learning from the Europeans as the Japanese had done was a better option. By the 1920s, China's best and brightest all looked to the West. They agreed that modern science and industrial capitalism was at the heart of Western success. But they could not agree how China could be united again after decades of civil war. In the end, the threat of dismemberment by foreign powers drove ideas of freedom and democracy into the shadows. Unification *at all cost* became the slogan that had the widest appeal. Young Chinese still wanted the secrets of modernity.

The only unease came from a nagging doubt that they would end up being imitation Westerners. To the Westerner, it was inconceivable that the Chinese could do anything except learn from them. The only question was how long it would take for them to become modern. China was no threat to the liberal ideas and institutions that made the world civilized.

Today that picture of the norm is being challenged. A new scenario is unfolding as "America First" takes center-stage in future transactions. There is less use of rhetorical weapons like democracy, human rights and the rule of law which some nations welcome, but the shift to negotiations based on national interests and skepticism towards multilateral agreements is unsettling. Xi Jinping's China was prepared to adapt to such transactional ways but he surprised those meeting at Davos when he affirmed support for the globalization project that brought peace and prosperity to the world. He put himself forward as an upholder of the ongoing system of interstate relationships. But if the United States wants deals that are primarily in its national interests, he knows that the approach would be based on calculations of relative power. That would lead to challenges of military strength where the US has immense advantages.

The idea that US supremacy might be severely diluted by a set of Asian powers is highly improbable. Chinese leaders recognize that. But the thought that this could happen might awaken the US to reinvent itself and revitalize its global role. That could lead it to lash out to stop the rising power while it has the military upper hand. In a scenario where it would lose its supremacy if it did not act, the ideal target is one that provides a lesson to all others. For now, the obvious target would be China, the only challenger whose political system also has a powerful economic base.

Xi Jinping and his colleagues are not so foolish to try to replace the United States as a dominant force. Newly rising powers like China and India could at best hope that a multi-polar order will be a better foundation for a durable peace. If they could persuade a less confident American superpower that multi-polarity would guarantee America's place in world affairs, there should be no need for alarm. If they fail, the defensive superpower would refuse to accept a lesser hegemony. The United States would choose to identify an evil enemy and play the role of a caring leader out to protect its allies. It could argue that only by so acting would the world stop the return to the anarchy from which countries have been trying to escape for decades.

Such worst-case scenarios where issues are black and white and solutions need swift solutions are too dangerous in a world with nuclear weapons. Chinese leaders have no illusions here. Their history shows that peaceful endings depended on leaders who mastered the art of the possible and knew when to seek the middle way of compromise. That way produced fewer undesirable outcomes but then the past suggests that there are only un-ideal endings to beautiful dreams. It does not mean that hopeful dreams should not be encouraged. The China Dream focuses on the hope that, staying with the globalization built by liberal market economies, China and the US could still try to be partners not only to persevere with the goals of the current world order but also to consider how that order could be reformed and modified.

IV. Not the Old Dream

The Dream of continuity with the past would take stock of the traumatic years of the 20th century. Chinese leaders know that blindly going forward will not produce any lasting answers. The country needs a set of anchors to ensure a degree of order and security. It also needs lessons for those who feel lost after two revolutions. While there is room for the universal and the cosmopolitan in everyone's life, people also need to be grounded in the local and comprehensible. Without that, they would not be able to move towards a modernity that they can relate to.

When the CCP won power 70 years ago, there followed a decade of questioning and confusion. Many Chinese had been exposed to different faces of the West but everyone was asked to follow the heresies of Marx and Lenin. Those who admired the mainstream ideologies of Western Europe and the US were expected to denounce those reactionary teachings. Outside the PRC, the Nationalists in Taiwan could survive only by backing anti-communist freedoms. Elsewhere, millions of overseas Chinese living in other people's new nations had to decide to whom they should be loyal. Very few Chinese anywhere had choices as to who they were. Only nation-states and the people who controlled them could determine what dreams they may have.

In 1971, the People's Republic of China was admitted into the United Nations. On the surface, China's leaders had never been surer of their position in the world. Mao Zedong's certainties about the CCP's future, about his political enemies within and the country's enemies without, were never stronger. No-one in China could disagree with that. Deep down, however, the people of China had never been more unsure as to who they were and where the country was heading. Abroad, the question was whether the United States or the Soviet Union was the greater enemy. Within the country, people thought the country had dumped Confucius into the dustbin of history. But the way he had to be denounced time and again must have made them wonder how true that was.

The return of Deng Xiaoping replaced that confused state with new hopes but also other unfamiliar uncertainties. The decision to open the country to the West was welcomed. The flood of scholars, students and officials who travelled to the West over the next decades was remarkable and they quickly transformed China's economy. Clearly, the West had more to teach China than the Soviet Union. It was more complex, variable and exciting and new ideas and institutions were introduced through books, magazines and the media at an unprecedented speed. Foreign universities had specializations in the fields of science, technology and the social sciences.Closer by, a great deal could also be learnt from other East Asian societies that had benefitted so much from the capitalist model of economic development.

Everything was either new or rediscovered, and the impact was instant among the bright young students who crammed into schools and colleges. The country could not build such institutions fast enough to cope with the rush in demand. Those with access could hardly be blamed for being carried away by the contrast between what they could read about the West for themselves and the negative images that officials and teachers still warned them against. The policy of opening-up young minds was close to revolutionary. Thus, when the Secretary-General of the CCP Hu Yaobang was sacked, this caused an uneasy pause and considerable disquiet. Issues of inflation and corruption led to tense inner-party struggles. When Hu Yaobang died in 1989, the demonstrations of grief brought out massive displays of dissatisfaction. This resulted in the tragedy at Tiananmen for many students and Beijing residents but it was also a severe setback for Deng Xiaoping's call to let more people learn from the West.

Then the Soviet Union collapsed and the Cold War ended. China was even more determined to master all it could to save what was left. The US revised its expectations of China now that it was triumphant and did not need China as an ally against Russia. Among Chinese, some began to divide between those who thought the West really wanted to help China develop and others who saw the West trying to thwart China's growth. Despite that, the expertise gained by Chinese people at all levels paid off and provided invaluable help to enable the country to manage its Western partners and competitors. It was this growing body of new skills and knowledge that made it feasible in 2017 for Xi Jinping to proclaim China's strong support for globalization. The line between liberal and illiberal was blurred and the idea of a non-Western order no longer inconceivable.

China is not offering its own version of universalism; instead, in the 18th Party Congress, the message was that of finding its own road to modernity. That road is centered on two pillars. Within the country, national sovereignty can be made safe only through social order and continued development, something only a united and well-organized party-state can guarantee. Outside, security is the goal. Here the conditions are more complex and its leaders know that there are many factors in the interdependent world that are beyond China's control. However, the country's integrity rests on the capacity to defend its borders even from the world's sole superpower.

Here Xi Jinping may agree with Deng Xiaoping that he should feel for the stones to help China cross to the other bank, but he seems also to be suggesting that some stones might be leading to wrong parts of that bank and therefore corrections are necessary. Of interest is that CCP leaders continue to refer to Marx as the guide to the country's future even when the country is committed to follow a modified capitalism to prosperity. The dream that China wants is not to replace the liberal order but to ensure that China's future is guided by modern compasses of its choosing. After the experiences of the past 150 years, that future would also require them to look back beyond the 20th century to the records of all their earlier dreams.

Chapter III

Navigating a Divisive Heritage

The China Dream has many components that require an understanding of China's past. This chapter will be in three parts. The first will explore the difficulties the Chinese people experienced in rebuilding the state. The second will explain how much that state derives its resilience from the tradition of keeping comprehensive collections of historical records. The third looks at the search for national identity and how it involves the integration of many sets of values in modern civilization. In order to bring the three aspects together, their leaders have to come to terms with complex questions of the power relations, moral leadership and legitimacy that had provided the country with its remarkable continuity.

Their efforts began in earnest when many of the May Fourth generation in the 20th century rejected every part of the country's past that came from the state orthodoxy of Confucianism. They looked for new ideas to help them determine what kind of republic was needed to replace the dynastic state. In particular, the new leaders found that the history of how nations emerged in Western Europe was especially relevant for people who have just discovered nationalism. Not least, they also wondered what mix of past and present ideas and institutions would enable the Chinese people to be modern and civilized.

The main outlines of the country's rises, falls and recoveries are well known and many books offer narratives of what happened over the past three millennia. But given the magnitude of the changes during the past century and the strong impact that China's recent changes are having, it is useful to review the significance of some of those narratives. This is my perspective of what might be included in any effort to reconnect with China's past.

For over 2,000 years, China has been an emperor-state in which many peoples with their different values and social systems were integrated by a centralized bureaucratic state. More recently, it was confronted by a different imperial system from Europe that was richer and more powerful. China's response was to abandon its dynastic state to establish a republic. Early in the 21st century, this new China regained its place as an economic power. What China has risen from and rising to become, and what China's evolving position means for the region and ultimately the world is the subject of endless debate today.

In the following sections, I look at key parts of China's heritage and at the efforts to draw on them to meet the needs of expanding skills and modernizing mindsets. While the historical developments experienced their changes at different times, all of them were interconnected: the kind of state best for China; the consistent use of official records in the process of renewal; the role that revolutions played in shaping the people; and the quality of their civilization.

I. Party-State

No one would deny that China had fallen precipitously during the past two centuries and that its attempts to recover from the fall were filled with tragedy. That was the result of the emperor-state's inability to defend itself against the dynamic nation-states of Europe that had extended their empires across the globe. I use emperor-state 皇朝 *huangchao* instead of the more common empire 帝国 *diguo* because that enables me to link the position of the emperor and his dynasty to the civilizational concept of *tianxia* 天下. The Qin and Han dynasties and their successors did not see themselves as monarchs of kingdoms. They claimed to be *tianzi* 天子 who received the mandate of Heaven and were higher than all kingdoms. In terms of military power and imperial reach, they were comparable to the Roman Empire and some other empires of the feudal ages but they defined their legitimacy differently.

(i) *The tianzi Syndrome*

The Chinese rulers claimed that it was their civilization that defined the state and guided their subjects to be loyal to the *tianzi*. That formulation was modified to allow more than one *tianzi* claimant from time to time, but the norm was that there should only be "one sun in the sky". The successive dynasties had their ups and downs, sometimes unifying and sometimes dividing the Chinese people. When they were strong, they evoked respect and fear; when weak and divided, they invited invasions. In time, the idea of the civilized Hua or Han imperial subjects as distinct from the tribal peoples around, the Hu, Rong, Yi and Man 胡戎夷蛮, came to define a superior people. But, without the legal concept of sovereign borders, this sense of identity did not develop into anything comparable to the Western European and now globally used concept of nationhood. For centuries, notably from the Tang dynasty, having a common written language and sharing the trinity of beliefs and practices of 儒、佛 and 道 (Confucian, Buddhist and Daoist) was enough to distinguish Chinese from others.

The relationship between China's ancient civilization and its political system was a complex one that changed many times. For over 2,000 years, the Han Chinese had to manage major cultural challenges while they dealt with tribal invasions by the ancestors of Turks, Mongols, Manchus and Tibetans. All of them left vestiges of their institutions that influenced the rulers who followed each foreign conquest. Many of the invaders had also accepted the Buddhism that was introduced into China from Central Asia and India. Together the mix of superior military organization and Buddhist doctrines strengthened the structure of state power and put traditional Confucian and Daoist loyalists on the defensive for at least five centuries through the Northern and Southern Dynasties down to the Tang dynasty. Those were years of extensive political and cultural change that also remade the social fabric from top to bottom. The new cultures changed the nature of military and aristocratic governance and enabled the state to determine the shape of Tang civilization. The imported ideas and institutions inspired generations of emperors and mandarins to rethink how the emperor-state should be organized. But the idea that the ruler was *tianzi* was retained.

There was nothing inevitable or predetermined about these changes. Different peoples and events contributed to the systems that evolved after the fall of the Han dynasty. What I have described as changes to the nature of the emperor-state were not necessary parts of a continuum. They were largely the results of specific responses to new conditions and reflected the capacity to adapt and change. Now that the modern globalization forces have become pervasive and irreversible, the Chinese are changing again. They are working under conditions where words like state, nation and civilization are used to explain what is China and who are Chinese. From the time when Sun Yat-sen and his supporters proclaimed the republic, Chinese leaders have been prepared to reinvent their past to shape a better future.

The first step was to replace the emperor-state of the *tianzi* with a nation of Chinese peoples ruled by the president. Words like *minzu* 民族, *Zhonghua* 中华 and *zongtong* 总统 were used to mark the new start. The revolution that pushed the Manchu *tianzi* to abdicate was represented by the word *geming* 革命 that traditionally referred to the overthrow of a failed dynasty. But this time, it was more radical and meant the replacement of a whole system of government.

This republic, headed by the president, consisted of elected representatives from all provinces of the country who chose the prime minister and his cabinet officers. Their duties and powers were laid down in a constitution approved by the national assembly. The system, with the separation of executive, legislative and judicial powers, broadly followed the American and French republics. Unfortunately, there was nothing constitutionally sanctioned about the agreement made between the "provisional president" Sun Yat-sen and Yuan Shikai, the Qing official to whom the Manchu emperor transferred his mandate. There were secret negotiations at the end of which the provisional government was moved from Nanjing to Beijing where Yuan Shikai was "elected" president. In fact, external recognition by the Great Powers through their embassies in Beijing was probably more important than anything else in conferring legitimacy to the new state.

It was an ominous beginning. The republic was little understood, not even by the man who was president. Having worked for the emperor-state all his life, he understandably wondered if the president was some kind of non-hereditary emperor. His actions displayed little understanding of the role of the assembly and, a year later, Sun Yat-sen's Nationalist Party withdrew support and launched an abortive "second *revolution*", further evidence that no one worried much about what words like revolution, constitution, separation of powers, political parties and cabinet government really meant. Equivalent Chinese words simply acquired new meanings as events unfolded.

Yuan Shikai could not see how the country could be without an emperor-like ruler and have a president who did not have comparable powers. After more frustrations, he dissolved the assembly, appointed his own supporters to serve an autocratic presidency and was persuaded by some of them that he might as well become emperor. It was a serious misjudgement. The opposition to his move was widespread among his own military cliques and he withdrew from the installation. A few months later in 1916, he died. From then to 1928, when the Nationalists won enough power in South China to establish a new government in Nanjing, the country was the battleground for a series of warlords. For many Chinese, divided China was subject to foreign manipulation and the lack of a strong central government meant that the Republic of China was a state of confusion.

There are some today who look back nostalgically to this period as one of considerable freedom for political activity, cultural and intellectual creativity, and private enterprise, especially in the Treaty Ports where some Chinese were able to share in the extraterritorial rights that foreign nationals enjoyed. Indeed, literature, the fine arts and education in the modern schools and colleges have been singled out as benefiting most from the lack of bureaucratic controls. But for those who asked who was running the country and how the Chinese state was defending the country and the economy, there was growing fear and disappointment. Not least prevalent was the sense that Chinese civilization was threatened and important cultural values at all levels of society were lost. Of particular concern was that alien ideas and institutions were eroding the civilization. Although few spoke of the call for "total Westernization" 全盘西化, much of the discourse on politics, philosophy, science and business was conducted freely by using the terminology and thought frameworks drawn from Europe, the US and modernized Japan.

In the context of state building, three models all employing Western ideological language attracted support. The first was the liberal democratic West identified with nationalism and capitalism; the second the internationalist socialism of the Soviet Union; and the third the new challenges from fascist and national socialist regimes in Central Europe. Behind each of the groups espousing these models were some voices reminding the people of their political heritage, the moral vision that Confucius and his disciples had gifted their ancient civilization.

Sun Yat-sen had begun with the first model. His more idealistic supporters went with it but the numerous warlords undermined it by battling incessantly to control the country. The man who eventually became Nationalist leader, Chiang Kai-shek, wanted to destroy his Communist rivals and turned to Nazi and Fascist countries for military assistance. The CCP leaders claimed to have been inspired by Marxist ideology but won the civil war by using a mixture of Leninist and Stalinist party organizational methods and Chinese traditions of peasant uprisings. After victory, Mao Zedong did use "continuous revolution" as a personal version of Marxism but the extreme methods he used were focused on acquiring total control of the authoritarian state that the CCP had established. The ideological slogans were superficial and irrational and had little to do with any known ideology.

In short, throughout the republican period and down to the end of the Cultural Revolution, Western ideas and methods were used to unify China by building a strong state. At its core, the common goal of both the Nationalist and the Communist leaders was to find a system to replace the emperor-state and provide China with the capacity to resist foreign dominance and establish order within the country. This was where the Communists were more successful in their use of an alien ideology. They had no illusions about the transfer of Western political values into the country but concentrated on methods that enabled them to rebuild a system that would empower China again.

(ii) *After Confucian Orthodoxy*

Let me go back to what the CCP went through to achieve this end. Mao Zedong set out to destroy traditional feudal values in the name of class struggle. That way he emphasized the creation of a new socialist era that displaced that of Chinese civilization. It is why, from 1949 till the early 1980s, there was almost a complete absence of books and essays that linked Confucianism to Chinese civilization. Mao Zedong was part of the generation that blamed China's woes on the Confucian emperor-state and sought to attribute all past achievements to the sweat, toil and genius of the ordinary people. He therefore encouraged historians to use Marxist stages of social progress to rewrite all of Chinese history and justify the total rejection of the dynastic system.

At the same time, he also condemned the values introduced from the West by people whom he considered bourgeois and cosmopolitan. Everything associated with capitalism and imperialism was fiercely criticized. By the 1960s, he went further and even the communist ideology introduced from the Soviet Union was subjected to severe attacks in the name of fighting revisionism. In this way, he was able to exercise unrestrained power to manipulate the superstitions and fears of the poorly educated young. By rejecting successively the Chinese feudal system, the liberal state of the American bourgeoisie and that of the Russian revisionists, there was little left of any kind of model for the new China to build on. He was left with a very basic worker-peasant-soldier understanding of life and work for which words like civilization and ideology were irrelevant.

It is therefore interesting that there was a revival of interest in past models in the 1980s after Deng Xiaoping's opening to the West. A large number of writings were published about a modern state being built on civilized values that condemned what had taken place during the previous decades. However, there was hesitation about what to do with China's own civilization. There remained a divide between those who admired the wisdom of their ancestors and those who wanted to construct a "socialist spiritual civilization" that would only draw selectively from that heritage. This resembled earlier searches for a better system for China: look to the liberal West, look to a socialism modified to suit China, but also look inwards to China's own time-proven values.

Whether communist or not, educated Chinese recognized that China had lost its cultural moorings. A whole generation had to start afresh to regain self-respect and a sense of national identity. For some, Deng Xiaoping's opening was like fresh water to thirsty throats. The new exposure to the various manifestations of modern life was exhilarating. In addition to European socialist books that had previously been suspect, there was a rush of new scientific and technological knowledge, together with unfamiliar social science theories and concepts and a backlog of experimental forms in every field of art and literature. Many began to consider how these might become cultural expressions that would help shape the modern Chinese state and therefore seen as values that the state would encourage.

The Chinese also saw how the Chinese who lived in Hong Kong, Taiwan and parts of Southeast Asia were free to construct their own worldviews in different frameworks. Those who had retained faith in Chinese traditions resurfaced and demanded a chance to re-educate the young for the new state. They believed that they could do better than the Chinese outside because, with their deeper roots in Chinese soil, what they could rejuvenate would have a greater authenticity.

The CCP was aware that the state it had established had failed to establish a stable environment for economic development. But revolutionaries like Deng Xiaoping and Chen Yun still believed that the socialism they had fought for was progressive. They were determined to learn from their mistakes and pursue reforms that would enable them to build a more effective state to pursue their ideals. They knew that they had lost time and China's economy had to grow quickly for the system to survive. There was no question of returning to the Confucian past or to Maoist utopianism. But they would also not risk the Party's future by allowing the free import of Western models of democracy that they believed would undermine the Party's authority.

At the same time, they knew that they had to satisfy the longings and ambitions of people who have been kept poor and suppressed for too long. It was in the context of these pressures that the new leaders mounted campaigns to link socialism with selected parts of China's cultural heritage, Western capitalist methodologies and Marxist ideas of progress. They believed that such a combination could provide the foundations of a modern state.

However, this vision was at best a clouded one. The problems for such a vision were revealed in the numerous writings published since the Tiananmen tragedy of 1989. The impact of the forces pressing for change could be seen in books and essays representing many points of view. These writings were significant because they were not produced under conditions of freedom but were what the censors have allowed. They showed what the new generations of intellectuals were able to do to push at the edges of creative thinking. They also illustrated the range of what the Party believed the state would need in order to be credible again.

One starting point was to re-examine how the state originated. Historians have confirmed that the artefacts unearthed since 1949 could trace its beginnings earlier than the written records. Hence the reference to 5,000 years of civilization that is in every textbook. What were found showed that being civilized originated with rituals and symbols that centred on an ancient written language. Over 3,000 years ago, the texts distinguished the *huaxia* 华夏 Chinese who developed that language from the *manmo* 蛮貊 tribes to the south and north who did not use it. The *huaxia* were those who used the language to promote and refine their state. By the time of Confucius, they were confident that the *manmo* within their state who adopted the language could become Chinese.

The scholars compared that ancient state with state-building else-where and looked for objective criteria to measure what made a state successful. They concluded that only civilized states became strong and resilient and acknowledged that there were several such states.

Some thought that the rich and strong destroyed or absorbed the poor and weak; others were ambivalent but agreed that those that have survived have much to offer the world because they are still able to evolve and grow.

China's ancient civilization was the product of small states that merged to become one strong state; the state then deepened and enlarged the civilization to protect and enhance its power. This was also true of the states in the West that had been shaped from different cultures and remained superior for over 200 years. Although most Chinese did not think that Western states are intrinsically superior, they recognized that their cultural values enabled them to command great wealth, scientific knowledge and power. To some, these values came from a superior ideology and that China also needed one that could serve as a unifying and overarching principle for the new state.

It is fascinating to see some scholars today returning to the ancient texts to seek a fresh understanding of the technologies and values that created the first states in China. Scholars like Yan Xuetong 阎学通, Ge Zhaoguang 葛兆光, Zhao Tingyang 赵汀阳, Wang Hui 汪晖 and Zhao Dingxin 赵鼎新 seem to be in the footsteps of scholars outside China like Qian Mu 钱穆, Xu Zhuoyun 许倬云 and Yu Yingshi 余英时 in pointing out the need to respect the past when rebuilding the state today.

From their writings, the rise of the monarchic system was connected with the body of classics that was used to examine candidates for public office. Eventually this evolved into the Neo-Confucianism that served as the state orthodoxy. By the Ming dynasty, the state decided that one set of classics should be widely spread through education as the mind and heart of the Chinese state. This was so successful that the literati class it produced thought that nothing else would be needed from outside China. When the Manchu Bannermen conquered China in 1644, they accepted the authority of this orthodoxy and continued to use it to control the Han Chinese majority and also provide legitimacy for Manchu rule. By allowing Han Chinese to act as protectors of the Confucian state, literati hostility was dissipated and Manchu emperors won their acceptance. As a result, the system was further consolidated.

The reasons why Manchu rule came to an end are complex. I favor the view that the Bannermen-literati system was destroyed by powers that were more advanced in every respect but also agree that the system self-destructed because it had become too conservative. For all concerned, the most important consequence was that the fall of the emperor-state had taken Chinese civilization down with it. When the Chinese elites of the 20th century sought an alternative to the failed state, they knew that they would also have to find another kind of civilization to help save China.

This is why so many books and essays on China's rise as a party-state return to the question of a future civilization linked to a "spiritual" side of socialism; they often added that this meant having Chinese characteristics. I shall discuss this further in Chapter 4. Here I note what the party-state thinks are important events to commemorate: for example, anniversaries like the centenary of the first Sino-Japanese War, the Hundred Days Reform, the Boxer Rebellion and the reforms that ended the examination system, and the considerable coverage of the 1911 Revolution. Also, the anniversaries of the May Fourth demonstrations, especially the 80th anniversary in 1999, 10 years after the Tiananmen tragedy. They reminded us that the republican state is still trying to discover the best ways to reconnect the present with the recent past.

The problem of reunification and failing to reunite continue to cast a shadow on the country. In many ways, this seems to have become more difficult because of the perception that the PRC has moved away from an emphasis on cultural identity to a party-state identity. This takes us back to the nature of the state that has been rebuilt. A compelling question for Chinese leaders is whether the state needs an ideology for its future development. During the Cold War period when the struggle between capitalism and communism was presented as paramount, Mao Zedong's calls for class struggle were loud and clear. They appeared to proclaim that a new ideology had replaced that of Confucianism.

The calls accused the old literati class of ruining the country with their reactionary shibboleths and celebrated its destruction. But the idea that China needed a new ideology survived and adopting Maoist ideals was a step towards producing a replacement. Many in the CCP felt that China could not recover its greatness if a new ideology was not forthcoming.

The sense of identity loss was linked to the loss of sovereignty in the Unequal Treaties, notably the legal and judicial rights granted to foreigners on Chinese soil. That had led to external capitalist control over most of China's industries and infrastructural developments. These condemned the Chinese to becoming employees and dependents in their own land. There followed other dimensions: the country remained divided for over 35 years and for most of that time hopelessly undefended. China survived largely because it was not in the interest of the Great Powers to allow any one power to dominate the stricken country. This gave many Chinese a sense of helplessness, in particular about their future as a civilized people. The loss of confidence in their moral traditions and the pathetic condition of their religious organization produced a sense of inferiority. Together, they undermined the efforts to build a strong state that could instil national pride.

The feeling of anguish was particularly marked among the Chinese intellectuals. Never in the history of China had its best and brightest experienced the virtual destruction of the very foundations of their heritage. As a result, there arose a wide range of emotions. They turned their anger onto those responsible for this loss, attacking those within and then seeking out those outside who had frustrated China's attempts to recover its place in the world. They became even more determined to fight to get China out of its tragic situation, and some also turned to soul-searching to tackle the causes that had led to such despair.

For those who abandoned the discredited traditions, they sought China's recovery by adopting ideas from the West, almost anything that could enable the new generations to change their fate. It did not matter which part of the West the ideologies came from as long as they produced the results that China wanted. What was remarkable was the consensus some of them reached to build the new *national* state. To them, that had become so important that, if the nationalists failed to achieve it, they were ready for yet another revolution to ensure the unity that could propel China to rise again.

II. Indispensable *Shi*-histories

I mentioned earlier that the republican state, the *hua* nation and the quest for a modern civilization all had to confront the country's long history. This meant having to face the test of modern historiography, and re-writing Chinese history was seen as one of the inescapable ways of starting afresh. China was not alone in having to respond to the dominant discourse in world history. All new nations established since 1945 have had to reconfigure their histories in the post-imperial framework created at the end of World War II.

But China found itself with a problem. Its emperor-state failed long before that Eurocentric framework became global. The republic that replaced it was alien, the product of the European Enlightenment. By accepting that institution, China also adopted the citizen base that gave the French and American republics their legitimacy. The French were already a nation while the United States saw itself as the first new nation building a world free from its British roots. Furthermore, the Chinese still believed that it had a great civilization long before the West was creating the modern one that it wanted the world to share.

One way to deal with this problem was to declare that their old Confucian foundations were no longer of any use and China had to start afresh to compete with the West and restore its wealth and power. The price was the loss of the continuity with its past, a condition that made its leaders pause. The price was too high, many thought. Was that really necessary, others asked? They could use part of their political traditions to build their republic. They could bring all the peoples within China's borders together in an enlarged *Zhonghua* nation.

In any case, how much continuity did China need to be the strong state that could unite the nation and support a distinctive civilization? If Chinese leaders could agree on that, what did they have to do to achieve that continuity? China's historians had begun to rewrite its history soon after the 1911 revolution. They placed China in the world history frame and assumed a linear chronology that divided the past into the ancient, the medieval and the modern. They then decided that China's modern history *jindaishi* 近代史 began with the Opium War of 1840.

This was different from the European modern that began in about 1500 following the discovery of the Americas. It also meant that Chinese history did not have the equivalent of the medieval *zhonggu* 中古. When 1840 was accepted as the start of modern history, the Chinese discovered that developments before 1840 were akin to some notion of ancient history *gudaishi* 古代史. Remarkably, the communist historians also accepted that the modern era began in 1840. Their Marxist justification for this periodization focused on the transition from capitalism to imperialism as a step on the road to socialism. Before that, for two millennia at least, all was "feudalism", an overarching condition that was both somehow *zhonggu* medieval and *gudai* ancient.

With almost everyone agreed that the Opium War marked the beginning of the modern history of China, the impact of the tradition of continuity was probably unexpected. The choice of 1840 became a real break with the *shi*-histories that had conceived of Chinese history in terms of dynastic periods. This tradition evolved from the Han dynasty and finally produced the comprehensive Four Treasuries (经史子集 *jing*-classics, *shi*-histories, *zi*-masters and *ji*-collections) Catalogue of the Imperial Library half a century before the Opium War, the *siku quanshu zongmu* 《四库全书总目》. Included in the *shi*-histories was the last *zhengshi* 正史 Standard History, that of the Ming dynasty covering the years 1368 to 1644. That was the 24th of the Histories that began with Sima Qian's *Shiji* 司马迁《史记》. Together, the 24 histories devised by official historians since the Tang dynasty were to ensure that there was no break in the Chinese past.

Thus, starting modern history from 1840 created two problems for the nationalist historians. If there was no medieval period, it made it extraordinarily difficult to deal with the idea of ancient history as a period of more than 3,000 years. And if the Chinese followed European usage and sub-divided an early modern period as 1500–1840, they could make little sense of the division between the Hongzhi 弘治 (1487–1505) and Zhengde 正德 (1505–1521) reigns in the middle of the Ming dynasty. As for the communist historians, they struggled endlessly to determine when the age of slavery (if it existed) gave way to that of feudalism and, in the end, stopped insisting on the Marxist periodization.

I shall not dwell on what Mao Zedong made of different kinds of peasant rebellions and how he discovered that China had produced early shoots *mengya* 萌芽 of capitalism during the pre-modern Ming-Qing period. Neither was helpful to the rewriting of Chinese history. Instead, it is interesting to follow the efforts to write a standard Qing history to cover the period 1644–1911.

This started with Qing loyalists who did the first version of *Qingshi* 清史 in the 1920s. That work was rejected by the Nanjing regime as poorly done, so it was only published as a draft history. Nothing else was done during the civil and anti-Japanese wars, but the idea persisted and a revised *Qingshi* was published in Taiwan in 1961. This was also unsatisfactory. Another attempt to compile a New *Qingshi* in 1991 came to nothing after the Guomindang lost the national elections in 2000. On the mainland, there had been several calls to write *Qingshi* but it was not until 2002 that a large team was gathered to compile it.

Why this persistence to get an officially recognized *Qingshi* written? The Qing loyalists did it as their duty when the republicans showed little interest. The nationalists in Nanjing were not enthusiastic but were concerned to follow tradition. In Taiwan, they acted because they did not want the communists to use it, if only symbolically, to claim a superior continuity with China's past. As for the communists, some were very interested but problems of economic disasters and political infighting distracted them for decades. When it was finally decided to go ahead, it was because Party leaders wanted the continuous features of China's history better understood. Among historians, not having a *Qingshi* to fill the 200-year gap from 1644 to 1840 has proved to be difficult to explain. What were Manchu achievements when the Qing was using Han Chinese resources? Would the filled gap not make reconnecting with China's past more credible?

There is an additional perspective on the role of *shi*-histories in China. It should not be confused with historiography. *Shi*-histories was identified in the Han dynasty as sets of books that Confucian scholars placed alongside the *jing*-classics that they considered the core texts of wisdom. *Shi*-histories grew in importance during the Tang and Song dynasties and came to represent a quarter of the total body of knowledge available to the emperor-state. This reached its apogee during Emperor Qianlong's reign when the catalogue of what the Imperial Library contained was produced. This showed *shi*-histories as a large body of records that illustrated policy successes and failures selected to assist future regimes to govern well. The records also served to confirm the value of the Confucian canon in providing guiding principles behind the policies and in training young literati mandarins to be good administrators.

This leads me to assess the place of *shi*-histories as necessary support for the Confucian canon and evidence of the emperor-state's resilience. It is often forgotten how difficult it was for the texts of the *jing*-classics to be fully accepted. The long process took over 1,000 years during which generations of literati explained, debated and reinterpreted the large body of knowledge that was accumulating around them. It was only during the Song dynasty between the 11th and 12th centuries that near-consensus was reached as to which texts should constitute the core of the *jing*-classics.

Confucian scholars have been using some of these texts since the 2nd century CBE to determine which core Chinese values should be recognized at the imperial court. Different generations of literati served the dynastic state and became indispensable to their rulers. This was not exceptional; there were other states and societies that valued their sacred books. Where there were established religions, the holy books also supplied the historical narratives that people needed to know. The rulers and scholars did not separate the works of wisdom from the records of political and economic events but saw the latter as meaningless without reference to the holy books. The best examples were countries with monotheistic religions like Judaism, Christianity and Islam where knowledge of the past was expected to conform to the revelations and truths in the holy books.

As for peoples who believed in many gods or manifestations of God, there were different ways of telling their history. Three traditions illustrate how ancient wisdom could be transmitted. Two come from

Indo-European language speakers and the third from the Sinitic peoples of what became China. Of the first two, one was shaped by those Indo-Europeans who came south, largely to North India and produced societies that were creative about whether to have gods or not. In North India, for example, the large body of Vedic scriptures rendered the idea of history irrelevant. The events that deserved remembering were dramatically preserved in works like the *Ramayana* and the *Mahabharata* where the accounts were combined with moral and political wisdom.

Other Indo-Europeans went westwards towards the Mediterranean. Their stories of gods were woven into poetry and drama as well as works of history. In particular, Greek and Roman philosophers produced worldly ideas, and their historians combined observation and narrative with analysis. After many tribulations from the fall of the Roman Empire to the Renaissance in Western Europe, they successfully combined with monotheistic Christianity to inspire the modern civilization that dominates the world today. Unlike in China, there was no hierarchy of knowledge in which history was formally recognized as second to the classics.

In ancient China, knowledge was in the hands of the literate at the power centers, the shamans and the aristocrats. We know little about their origins before the Zhou dynasty (11th century BCE) but under the Zhou, the literate elites who served a loose assembly of states were free to present their views and engage in disputations. By the middle of the first millennium, in the numerous states of the Spring and Autumn period, learned men offered advice to any ruler who would listen as to how states should be governed. The most prominent shaped the schools of thought that dominated moral and political discourse for at least three centuries. Among them was Confucius. He was the first to refer to the Six Classics *liujing* 六经 or *liuyi* 六艺, and advocated that people who wish to serve the rulers must study these texts. The six were the *Books of Change, Poetry, History, Music, Rites,* and *the Spring and Autumn Annals Yi, Shi, Shu, Yue, Li, Chunqiu* 《易》、《诗》、《书》、《乐》、《礼》、《春秋》. Because the *Book of Music* was lost, later references were to the Five Classics.

Other rival schools after Confucius all knew of the six books but did not endorse them. The wide range of their writings testified to the innovative thinking that was taking place during the last centuries of the Zhou. But, after the Qin unification established an imperial *tianxia*, the dominant school of *fajia* 法家 Legalists subjected all other writings to close scrutiny. The Qin emperor ordered some texts to be destroyed, notably the *Book of History* from which Confucians drew their principles of governance.

The Han successors did not depend on the Legalists and experimented with other ideas, leading to the fourth emperor Wudi's invitation to Confucian scholars like Dong Zhongshu 董仲舒 to help him run the empire. Thus were the Five Classics revived. This was not without controversy. The authenticity of the texts and the different interpretations were debated for centuries. But as long as Confucians remained prominent in imperial service, what they deemed as classics remained the centre of scholarly attention.

After the Han, there were several rival claims for official recognition as classics, including works outside the governance structure, for example, those of Laozi and Zhuangzi as Daoist classics and the Buddhist sutras introduced from India. But those educated in the Confucian classics continued to administer the Legalist state institutions that were operative during three centuries of division before the reunification under the Sui and Tang dynasties. The image of the oneness of *tianxia* was then endorsed through the sets of *shi*-histories that were authorized early in the Tang. These included the *shu*《书》that consisted of records and documents from the Han to the Tang dynasties and were largely compiled by Confucian officials. The decisive moment was when the Tang set up the History Office in the 7th century to keep faithful records systematically of everything the emperors said and did, and collected and edited all documents as aids to good governance.

Scholars have been organizing books into different categories from the Han dynasty, but it was not until the Tang dynasty that the four categories were officially recognized as classics, histories, masters and collections. What each contained, however, was subject to change, and many additions and omissions were made over the centuries. The major changes were in the classics category where only Confucian texts and their interpretations, annotations and commentaries were included. The Four Treasuries catalogue made clear that in the Imperial Library books was all the knowledge that the Confucian state needed. Also obvious was the supremacy of the *jing*-classics and the supporting role of *shi*-histories. That had not always been so.

(i) *Providing Continuity*

Han Confucianism was only one of several contenders for imperial attention and its adherents had to work with allies among the Legalists, Daoists and members of the Five Elements and Yinyang School. During the centuries of division from the 3rd to 6th centuries, Buddhist *jing*-sutras and some Daoist classics supplanted the Confucian texts; some of them were more influential down to at least the 10th century. While Confucians continued to hold important administrative positions, their classics were important only to a small circle. Even the Confucians had to read other writings for their enlightenment, and there was also great admiration for fine prose and poetic skills, and for the practical arts of astronomy, medicine and war. However, it was during the Tang dynasty that commoners could gain public office through a more open examinations system. In that way, a literati group began to grow and gain influence at the court. These mandarins began to pick out those *jing* texts that provided the best training for future generations of officials.

In the meantime, the compilation of *shi*-histories gained authority among those ambitious to serve their emperors. Great attention was paid to methods of research and authentication, the beginnings of what we call historiography. In particular, specialists assigned to work in the History Office were tasked to ensure that the lessons needed for effective administration were clear. Conscious of the need for accuracy, men like Liu Zhiji 刘知几 in his *Shitong* 《史通》 *General History* also sought a higher historical sensibility. His work inspired Du You 杜佑 to compile his encyclopaedia of governance *Tongdian* 《通典》 *Authoritative Records*, and later also Wang Pu's 王溥 two sets of *Huiyao* 《会要》 Institutional history.

Together with the Seventeen *zhengshi Standard Histories* compiled by the 11th century, they led to the great Song compilations, the *Zizhi tongjian* 《资治通鉴》 *Mirror for Government*, the *Tongzhi* 《通志》 *Comprehensive Records*, and the *Wenxian tongkao* 《文献通考》 *Comprehensive Examination of Documents* that, each in its own way, covered all of Chinese history to the end of the Five Dynasties in 960 CE. These records, and also hundreds of other documentary collections, provided an increasingly strong sense of continuity that bound each dynasty to the whole length of China's history. Furthermore, they provided evidence wherever they could to confirm that the *jing*-classics had taught sound principles for successful government.

As noted earlier, it had taken many centuries to arrive at a consensus about what the *jing*-classics were. While the contents and significance of each text were being debated, the historical records continuously played their important role for the emperor-state. In describing what each dynasty did, they collectively supported and reaffirmed the validity of the classical texts. They provided indispensable evidence that the *jing*-classics (beginning with Six and later expanded to Thirteen) should be compulsory learning for aspiring functionaries. Adding the store of other philosophies and methodologies of the *zi*-Masters and of the literary and practical literature in *ji*-Collections, the total knowledge available to the literati gave them both intellectual satisfaction as well as the confidence that China was truly civilized.

Chinese literati-mandarins lived with this certainty ever since the latter half of the Song dynasty and saw that body of knowledge as a source of strength for their civilized state. At the same time, that official class became over-confident and complacent; this was one of the reasons why they failed to keep up with the developments after 1500 among the restless and aggressive people of Western Europe.

(ii) *For a Socialist Realm*

The China Dream expects to connect with China's past while trying to be a part of the new world order. Does it need to replace a dysfunctional orthodoxy with a set of modern texts? Xi Jinping had grown up with

Mao Zedong's vision of a continuous class struggle as the basis of new ideology and would not want to return to that nightmare. He then worked for three decades in support of Deng Xiaoping's reforms; and under Jiang Zeming and Hu Jintao, he saw them reaching out to China's recent past and tentatively seeking connections with the Confucian heritage. Does he hope that his Thought on Socialism with Chinese Characteristics for a New Era could be the new ideology to replace the state Confucianism dismissed a century ago?

He knew that a republican constitutionalism did not work. Although the nationalists in Nanjing acted quickly to install *Sanmin zhuyi* as a substitute for the *sishu wujing* 四书五经 classics, the texts did not inspire the people. He would also know how long it took for Confucian texts to become the *lixue* 理学 classics accepted as the source of Chinese core values. This would suggest that he does not expect Xi Jinping Thought to make an impact quickly.

The Republic of China battled decades of political division and economic impoverishment without an accepted set of classics. The PRC endured nearly 30 years of intra-party conflict without settling on any workable doctrines. Since then, it has done exceptionally well without an established ideological framework. What is more, the Soviet model it copied came to a humiliating end, and communism as the beacon of light and hope has become faint for CCP loyalists and has faded altogether for the Chinese people.

The key factor that kept China going in the past century were entrepreneurial and adaptable people willing to accept hardship and willing to learn. Somehow the political system, even under unpredictable leaders, managed to grow stronger after several disruptions. Despite challenges from hostile foreign interests, the leaders rebuilt the centralized bureaucratic state and made progress in redefining the nation. Again and again, they experimented with new ideas for the country's future while also asking how they might reconnect with the historical experiences that had made China great.

Xi Jinping can look back at the PRC's experiences since 1949. The idea that there should be a guiding ideology backed by a set of canonical classics led them to the writings of Marx, Engels, Lenin and Stalin.

During the Cultural Revolution, the Mao analects in the *Little Red Book* became holy mantra accompanied by 10 years of destruction and hysteria. What good did that do apart from eliminating anyone who disagreed and eliminating some of the best-educated minds that had responded to the promise of New China?

Deng Xiaoping survived the irrationalities and sought practical solutions to urgent problems. He eschewed ideologies and concentrated on devising workable policies; the idea of pinpointing a set of classical texts faded into the background. He changed direction altogether and exhorted his comrades to reserve their energies to perform well and produce results. He encouraged the people to believe in themselves and to be open to the benefits of global pluralism. But when he thought that some of them, especially the young, had become over-enthusiastic and ideological about the liberal values of the West, he cracked down mercilessly. He reminded them of his hopes for socialism with Chinese characteristics but refrained from imposing any kind of *jing*-classics on the country.

At the same time, he did not prevent debates on why China needed theory *lilun* 理论. He understood the value of guiding principles that drew not only from Western and Chinese history but also from successful practice. The debates showed that most people no longer believed that there was any ready-made model that also provided a set of canons. The world has advanced beyond that stage and continues to change so rapidly that such an approach is bound to lead nowhere. Some texts may stimulate thinking and should be read more carefully than others but the main thrust of the modern and innovative, the role of the new state and the core of national interest must not depend on any bundle of texts.

Furthermore, no one expects China to copy everything from the West. After a century of disputes, it is clear that only by becoming a better China would satisfy its people and enable them to make progress. Now that China understands what science and economics can do, the country needs to return to the quality of relationships that make for a stable and harmonious society that learns from the mistakes of the past, including lessons from having deviated from an older wisdom.

This brings me back to the Chinese rediscovery of its past and being awoken to the value of continuity if the country is to anchor its current rapid development to the qualities of resilience in their inheritance. In the past, their *jing*-classics was always tightly paired with *shi*-histories; without the latter's guarantee of continuity, the *jing*-classics might not have survived. Now that Chinese leaders have yet to find a new set of classics, their grasp of what *shi*-histories had done for China would be even more vital to its future.

Chinese historians know that *shi*-histories were not limited to what is studied in modern historiography (历史学) or the academic discipline of history. *Shi*-histories were compendia that consisted of the totality of history, geography, economics, law, sociology, government and public administration — just about every set of skills that straddle the humanities and social sciences today. Understanding this role of *shi*-histories would illuminate the way that practical knowledge had enhanced the quality of China's state, society and economy. It would also remind us that it was but one of a four-part framework in which there was keen respect for the *zi*-Masters and its wide range of mental and manual skills as well as the *ji*-Collections where the creative and aesthetic energies of the Chinese people were on show. The modern mind would appreciate how innovative ideas and original scientific methodologies have also been derived from learning from those who came before.

There is, however, one concern that needs attention. Many Chinese believe that continuity with China's long history was the key to their distinctiveness as a civilization. As suggested earlier, there was a significant gap in that story. I refer to the periodization that identified modern Chinese history as beginning in 1840 and left a curious gap between 1644 and 1840. The desire to complete a credible history of the Qing dynasty reminds us of this distinctiveness in Chinese self-knowledge. When *jing*-classics were not determined, the series of *shi*-histories constructed the frame of institutional memory. In that way, it also confirmed the perennial value of the *jing*-classics.

This experience endorsed the belief that knowledge of the past was the key to good governance and was almost like saying that good governance was the end of history. Many thought leaders in China, including Xi Jinping and his close advisers, seem to have come round to the view that the continuum between past and future is the norm. They are committed to excel in science and technology, in finance and entrepreneurship, in order to make the country strong and prosperous. They may now find that replacing the *jing*-classics would be difficult and perhaps unnecessary. But they appear to realize that, unless they understand the role of historical knowledge in documenting the falls and rises of China, they will not grasp the meaning of the changes the country has been through and the changes it still has to face. Without that understanding, it will be difficult to build a modernity that Chinese people can be proud of.

III. National Civilization

How the Chinese leaders have been treating their heritage in modern times suggests that they had no wish to return to the past. They faced the challenge to become a nation-like state in a world where there are many kinds of such states. They knew that China could not simply copy the Western European models of the 19th and 20th centuries. But the country needed a national identity to protect the country's sovereignty. It needed modern citizens with the capacity to remain civilized.

The 1911 revolutionary nationalists were aware that people who had long been subjects owing loyalty to the dynastic state would find the concept of citizenship incomprehensible. What the people were told was that, after the fall of the Qing dynasty, all who lived within its borders were now some kind of *hua* 华 Chinese. In 1949, the PRC confirmed that all who lived within the international borders of China, including the Han, the Manchu, the Mongol, the Tibetan, the Uighur and some 50 other minority groups, had Chinese nationality.

But many both inside and outside the country continued to ask questions about how to define a nation with so many non-Han minorities. Two examples illustrate some obvious anomalies and remind us of situations that are peculiar to China. One of them dealt with an issue of historical interpretation that went against the power of popular perception. The other comes from China's periphery on the island of Taiwan where people of Chinese are contemplating new ideas of nationhood.

The first concerns the famous general of the Southern Song dynasty, Yue Fei, who was glorified by the Chinese during the Sino-Japanese War of 1937–1945 as an archetypal patriotic hero. For decades, the poem *Manjianghong* 满江红 attributed to Yue Fei provided most of the words for one of China's most famous songs. He was described as someone with national pride who defied the mandarins and fought the Jurchen Jin 金 armies coming from North China and Manchuria. For his bravery and being wrongly jailed and executed, he became a popular hero among ordinary Chinese. After the Mongols conquered China, his status rose even further and, during the Ming and Qing dynasties, it acquired god-like characteristics.

Both those dynasties recognized that Yue Fei was popularly admired but focused attention on his exemplar loyalty to his Emperor Song Gaozong. The Manchu Qing rulers were particularly sensitive about whom he fought against. As descendants of the Jurchen tribes whose Jin dynasty armies were the enemies that Yue Fei defended the Song against, they carefully deflected the admiration for Yue Fei to emphasize his loyalty to the dynasty and depicted him as the general who sacrificed himself to protect his emperor. However, these attempts could not displace the popular view of him as a patriotic Chinese who resisted barbarian invaders.

With the republic, Yue Fei was promoted as a nationalist patriot. During the 1930s, there was a campaign to compare the Japanese to the Jurchen invaders. Yue Fei's exhortations to defend the country were likened to Chiang Kai-shek's calls for national defence. But, after 1949, new questions were asked about the nature of his heroism. The answer was that the Jurchen were ancestors of the Manchu, the Manchu are now part of the *Zhonghua* nation, and the Jurchen were also Chinese. Therefore, Yue Fei's battles against them could not be described as patriotic. This revision of Yue Fei's place in history went against his popular image and many people objected. So the authorities decided to relegate the topic to academic debate and not use it to define national identity. This episode showed that it was difficult to project a modern political concept backwards to change an entrenched view.

The other example is from Taiwan. Recent developments are challenging what most people mean by being Chinese. Many who do not want Taiwan to become part of the PRC have insisted that they are not Chinese. They may agree that their *guoyu* National Language is Chinese and Taiwanhua (derived from southern Fujian dialects) is also Chinese. But there are calls for people to "de-*sinify*" 去中国化 or turn away from Chinese *national* identity.

The contradictions are manifest. *Guoyu* has been the language of government and education since 1945. It was a matter of pride that the written Chinese and the knowledge and understanding of traditional Chinese culture among scholars there were better than those on the mainland. For a while, the elites in Taiwan saw themselves as standard-bearers of Chinese civilization with a strong claim to be the true China.

It is tempting to compare their efforts to construct a new imagined community with various kinds of nation building in post-colonial Asia. They point to the fact that the island was never part of China until the Manchu conquered it in 1683. The PRC government, on the other hand, saw Taiwan as the last corner of China that held out in the course of a civil war. That status was enhanced by the magnificent Palace Museum collection in Taipei that marked the authenticity of the Chinese heritage in the most visible way.

The two examples are reminders that *minzu* nation is a difficult word to pin down. One of the difficulties came from the fact that most foreigners, and even many Chinese themselves, use the word Chinese to refer to the Han majority. As long as that continues, the non-Han minorities of China are by definition not Chinese. The republican state, however, use *Zhongguoren* to translate Chinese, applying the word to all nationals of *Zhongguo* (whether the PRC or the Republic of China). That way, the Han is only the largest among 55 other groups of Chinese. *Zhongguoren* share a common territory and history, learn the same written language and are expected to hold similar sets of beliefs and practices. They are deemed to have national attributes comparable to those of other nation-states.

The republican state acknowledged that large minorities like the Tibetan, the Uighur and the Mongol did not see themselves as Chinese. Some foreign scholars have argued that China was a land-based empire that should meet the same fate as other empires like the Ottoman, Austro-Hungarian and Soviet empires and be dismantled following the end of the empire. That approach suggests that the Chinese claim to be a nation will always be critically scrutinized and could be seriously challenged if the country should become weak again.

Earlier in this chapter, I explained why some Chinese leaders came to think that the 1911 revolution was not enough and that China needed another one to give it a social transformation appropriate to a modern nation. As someone who was born and brought up in foreign empires established by powerful nation-states, I found that people like me found it easy to understand what Sun Yat-sen and the nationalists wanted for China. The idea of nation for Chinese overseas highlighted the fact that most of them were living in somebody else's national empire. For those in China, they were used to being imperial subjects and were brought up to accept the concept of *tianxia*. Thus when the nationalists announced that China was a nation, everything turned out to be more complicated than they expected.

Where Sun Yat-sen's republic was concerned, the Great Powers were not agreed that it should be recognized as a nation-state. Qing China was to them an empire and, like other empires, subject to the principle of self-determination for those peoples within it who could demonstrate their potential to be separate nations. This principle raised the hopes of minorities like the Mongols, Tibetans and Uighurs who had always argued that they owed allegiance to the Manchu Qing rulers but their lands had never been part of China.

Chinese nationalist leaders refused to accept that right of self-determination. Their state was built on different legitimacy principles and they were not subject to an international system that China had no part in creating. Whether in Beijing, Nanjing or Guangzhou, the leaders all agreed to trace the relationships between the Han and the various

Mongol, Tibetan and Uighur Turk to the concept of *tianxia* that connected them all. In that context, they followed the late Qing formulation of China as the Great Harmony of Five Peoples 五族大同 (other wordings included United Five Peoples 五族合一 and the Five Peoples Family 五族一家). Because the nationalist leaders advocated a republic in 1911, they modified the concept to refer to the Republic of Five Peoples 五族共和. They then went further to define the Five Peoples as core members of the *Zhonghua minzu* 中华民族, *Chinese* peoples that included many others living within the country's borders.

They acknowledged that this concept was different from the narrowly conceived idea of nation-states used in Western Europe. Sun Yat-sen, for example, contended that this idea of *minzu* was appropriate for peoples who were agrarian and pastoral and had interacted for so long across China's vast land areas. He was confident that when the various peoples became united as one and the country became more industrialized, urbanized and modern, the Chinese nation would be comparable to the developed nations in the West. Other leaders were less clear about what they understood by the idea of a nation-state and this remains a debatable issue in China today.

Those who have joined in the conversation admit that China's transformation to a modern nation-state is still work in progress. The plural concept of the nation was rooted in the emperor-state. As described in Chapter 2, that state was a centralized bureaucratic administration under an authoritarian ruler, justified as essential for a large and dispersed society consisting of a variety of peoples with distinctive cultures. It was assumed that, as long as the country was largely one of rural peasantry, it would have been difficult not to depend on this authoritarian system. The system rested on the cosmic authority of *tian* Heaven that mandated the founders of each dynasty with the right to rule with unchallenged power. One key reform after the system was established was to soften the Legalist structure and employ learned men to provide moral purpose and gain wider acceptance from the peasantry. The Han Empire introduced new criteria for selection through examinations and established basic ideals of meritocracy.

In this way, Confucian scholars were brought in to advise the rulers, educate young princes and train future officials to serve the emperor-state. In doing this, they also developed a set of *li* 礼 Rites that took precedence over appeals to the *fa* 法 law codes. More fundamentally, the Confucians placed high value on the family as the basic unit of a harmonious society and portrayed the Son of Heaven as the head of a large household who presided above all earthly and man-made institutions. In addition, they emphasized that Heaven could still intervene as the final arbiter. The emperor-family would no longer be legitimate if its leaders failed to provide for their family-subjects or failed to defend the ancestral lands. The state was thus seen as the family-*tianxia* 家天下, one that acted to preserve the interests of the dynastic house. This made the state the emperor's family realm. The Confucian doctrines were transmitted from one dynasty to the next. This system of governance managed by Confucians evolved to serve the different needs of successive dynasties and enabled each of them, whatever its ethnic origins, to be legitimate. Heaven was thus not a Han Chinese monopoly. The Confucians who made the system work could also be non-Han. Nothing they did encouraged the Chinese to develop a sense of nationhood.

How is this still relevant to the question of political legitimacy today? We know that the nationalist revolutionaries rejected this Confucian order, although there were still some who believed that some Confucian ideals should be retained. Serious divisions arose between those who led the political revolution and those who thought it did not go far enough and that a social and cultural revolution was what China really needed. But, from the struggles that followed, a few issues seem to have been agreed by them all. At all cost, the country had to be united again and order and stability restored. To achieve that end, there seemed to have grown a common willingness in both the GMD and CCP to accept that the state must be a powerful central authority under strong leadership.

How this was to be achieved was tied to the question of how to enable the republican state to build a Chinese nation. The revolutionary elites believed they could do so in a more caring way than the previous regime. They represented legitimacy in the name of new concepts like *guomin* nationals and *gongmin* citizens 国民 and 公民. It is interesting to see how, in different ways, leaders like Sun Yat-sen and Chiang Kai-shek and then CCP leaders from Mao Zedong to Deng Xiaoping to Xi Jinping used this to support the party-state and make it the successor of the emperor-state.

This party-state is not the one-party state familiar in Western political science literature. Party here does not mean one part of, or even the dominant party in, the nation. Where there are 56 "nationalities" and the idea of a single *zhonghua* 中华 nation is not fully recognized as one people, the party can serve as a useful substitute to act as the country's unifying political identity, the party-nation. I shall come back to the idea of party-nation later. Here I return to where the multi-national republic began and how it evolved in response to global developments.

The Manchu elites and the Han literati worked closely together, especially during the 19th century. While they distinguished Man 满 from Han 汉, they did not necessarily equate that with Man ruler and Han subject. The Qing emperor-state therefore was not a *national* empire like those established by European nation-states. Nation-states in the West allowed each country to project itself as a united citizenry that could be mobilized for national aggrandizement. That unity of purpose made them far more efficient than the Qing and other similar empires that consisted of many nationalities.

The early republic, the Nanjing government and the Maoist revolution each made sharp breaks with the imperial past in its own way. But they all depended on military victory and it was taken for granted that victory was enough. But in the international system, more important was the external recognition given by other nations before the regime could be confirmed as legitimate.

This was an issue with the first revolution — the question of the succession from Sun Yat-sen to Yuan Shikai in March 1912. Sun Yat-sen's forces had not won a decisive victory, but neither could Yuan Shikai win wars in southern China. There was thus a stalemate. For the foreign legations in Beijing, they saw no reason to recognize the revolutionary government and its provisional president in Nanjing as long as the Manchu emperor was still on the throne. Yuan Shikai was acting on behalf of the court and in a strong bargaining position to demand that the revolutionaries give up their claims to be the new government. In Beijing, he was well-placed to force the Manchu ruling elites to agree to abdication.

Even more important, Yuan Shikai controlled the capital and almost all the northern provinces, and the emperor was the *tianzi* to whom the peoples of Mongolia, Tibet and Xinjiang-Turkestan owed allegiance. The nationalists wanted the entire Qing heritage to become the new republic. Therefore, they realized it was wise to keep the capital in Beijing to make sure that all the non-Han territories were recognized as Chinese territories.

This was crucial when foreign recognition was not forthcoming. The embassies in Beijing were skeptical of Sun Yat-sen's legitimacy while the Manchu handover to Yuan Shikai seemed genuine. It was feared that any uncertainty in the republic's authority would have triggered Russian, British and Japanese military interventions in Mongolia, Xinjiang, Tibet and in Manchuria itself. But most historians agree that, above all Sun Yat-sen gave up the presidency and Yuan Shikai accepted it because of a distribution of military power in the Chinese provinces.

(i) *The Promise of Revolution*

I return to the word *geming* before it was used to translate the modern idea of revolution. Used within the Chinese realm, it represented the legitimate result of a just civil war. The word was later extended to include non-Han invaders who overcame Han rulers and won the mandate to rule over northern parts of China. By the 14th century, Ming historians had to decide whether *geming* was appropriate to apply to the Mongol conquerors. To do so would have stretched the original idea of righteous victory blessed with a mandate to rule. The Yuan historians had earlier blurred the issue by compiling *shi*-histories (including Standard Histories) for the Khitan Liao and Jurchen Jin dynasties together with the Song. Then followed the rather perfunctory compilation of similar *shi*-histories to cover the Mongol period.

This suggests that the *shi*-histories were now less about celebrating righteous mandates than about transmission of policies and institutions that were worth recording. The records of Mongol rule were dutifully selected to fill the gap between the Song and Ming dynasties. When the Manchu replaced the Ming, they did the same. Here the Han Chinese mandarins involved were more conscientious about teaching future mandarins the right lessons and took great pains to produce a respectable collection. *Geming* did not receive contemporary attention; it had become a term of historical interest.

Thus when the Japanese adopted the word to translate the modern idea of revolution, rebel leaders like Sun Yat-sen were quick to see how *gakumeisha* 革命者 could apply to their modern revolutionary cause as well as connect them with the just and mandated cause the word described. Sun Yat-sen in particular was very proud to wear *geming* as a badge of honor.

By equating *geming* with their revolution, the nationalists had raised their opposition to the emperor-state to a higher political goal and began to think in national terms. They soon found that it was not straightforward. There was much confusion as to where authority rested, Yuan Shikai's presidency or the national assembly consisting of representatives from every province. In the confusion, the assembly was dissolved in 1914. The nationalists drew back to the southern provinces and turned to local forces to resist the powerful warlords who had already carved out key northern provinces. This was back to the battle for the mandate to rule by winning on the battlefield. The word *geming* acquired a Janus-face quality; it could be used to look forward towards a progressive future and at the same time help Chinese leaders to reconnect with their political heritage.

This bifocal goal of *geming* described the new reality whereby political parties offered inspiring principles that could determine the structure of power. Sun Yat-sen had come a long way. He had begun by calling upon traditional secret societies and his Christian friends and sought support from like-minded intellectual and student activist groups. As he progressed, he was even more eclectic; he turned to European, American and Japanese models to find ways to control his political allies. He was determined not to revert to any kind of monarchy, and none of his colleagues would contemplate becoming emperor. Therefore, he was free to consider what kind of party and leadership could save China.

Sun Yat-sen's credentials as a nationalist were not in question, but that was not enough if he did not have an army to help him achieve his revolutionary goals. In fact, not having his party's army was a liability because money received from supporters was often wasted on unreliable soldiers led by former Qing officers. After World War I, when his position was at its weakest, he was attracted by the success of the Russian Revolution and saw a new opening to explore.

Sun Yat-sen had not been interested in Marxism, nor was he convinced that Lenin's interpretations of Marxism for Russia would ever suit Chinese conditions. But he was impressed that the Bolsheviks were able to use the forces under their control to seize power and then fight off the foreign armies sent to destroy them. When Moscow sent representatives to establish contact, the nationalists saw that, if they were to have any chance to succeed, they would have to do something similar. They accepted Soviet advice to re-structure the party and help train a party army. They even allowed CCP members to join their party.

Thus was created the party-army that laid the foundations of the party-state in China. Sun Yat-sen did not live long enough to do much, but his followers established the new regime in Nanjing in 1928 with his party and army in full charge. By that time, legitimation by foreign powers was easier. Warlord anarchy had undermined the country's stability to the point that even the Western embassies in Beijing were prepared to give the Nationalists a chance. To them, Chiang Kai-shek's military victory was credible enough to gain their recognition.

Unfortunately for the Nationalists, their capacity to control China was limited to its eastern and central provinces. The party became bitterly divided and Chiang Kai-shek took charge as head of the party-army. The Nanjing regime gained only the nominal allegiance of the warlords in the west and north; others in the south only paid lip service to the national government. Also, in the course of the Northern Expedition, the Nationalists had turned against their CCP partner; this turned made the communists their deadly enemies for the next two decades.

By that victory, the party fulfilled the conditions of legitimacy. But it did not want a Heaven-approved emperor, nor accept the army commander's right to rule. Chiang Kai-shek's political credentials were weak and, in the intra-party struggles that followed, his efforts to obtain greater control of matters of state led him to be called dictatorial. In time, his opponents, especially his communist enemies, mocked the regime as having replaced the imperial family realm of *jiatianxia* with the party realm of *dangtianxia* (党天下).

It probably mattered little at the time to be thus called. The *geming* process had made them legitimate. When the CCP with its People's Liberation Army (PLA) led the *second* revolution to displace the Nationalists, it was the CCP's turn to establish its own party-state. This was a major change insofar as the CCP led a socio-political revolution that was fought to give the people social justice. That claim to connect *geming* with justice received internal acceptance by most Chinese after the Nationalists moved to Taiwan. Abroad, although opinions were divided, the first decade of party-state rule was widely seen as successful.

However, the most convincing legitimacy was derived from having reunified the country after 38 years of disorder. In addition, this new *geming* set out to create a united nation, something the Chinese people had never known. Most Chinese began to feel strongly about nationalism from the 1930s onwards following the existential threat from Japan. That had convinced many to accept the party-state as the instrument for strengthening China. They would expect such a state to build a long-lasting system comparable to the emperor-state, one that would bring power and wealth to China.

Much will depend on how the CCP can reform itself to meet this rising consciousness. What is intriguing is that, given the difficulties the country has faced in trying to shape a unified Chinese nation, a united and disciplined national party that recruits from the best and brightest may well be the representative institution of the country. If a law-abiding and incorruptible meritocracy endures, the party could become the authority that defines the quality of the nation. That leads me to ask whether the party-state as Chinese nation could produce a civilization that is different not only from what the Chinese people have known from the past but also from what the rest of the world might be expecting.

(ii) *Enlarging the Social Base*

At the same time the Chinese were negotiating their way to a sovereign multi-nation, they faced a tough challenge: how to be modern and civilized and still be Chinese. Here they encountered an idea of civilization as a mission to civilize the world that challenged their notion of civilization as a shared possession. There is a significant gap between the idea of *mission civilisatrice* and that of *tianxia weigong* 天下为公 a world shared by all.

In scholarly writings, tracing how humans came to be civilized in different ways has enabled us to understand how we progressed from the ancients to the moderns. It was in the 18th century European age of enlightenment that the word "civilization" was retrospectively used to highlight the achievements of the Egyptians and Babylonians down to the Anglo-French North Atlantic. The word was introduced to measure higher stages of human attainment with special reference to developments arising out of city living. Since then, it has acquired multiple meanings.

The Chinese were introduced to the concept of *wenming* 文明 used by the Japanese in the translation of Francois Guizot's (1787–1874) *History of Civilization in Europe*. Scholars like Liang Qichao and Zhang Binglin were attracted by the state-building successes that made people civilized. They were impressed by the modern search for objective criteria to measure what was civilized or not. This included the idea that civilized states became strong and set the standards for mankind. Like the Japanese, many Chinese scholars were inspired to re-examine the civilization they partially shared if only to affirm that they too were civilized.

This was also the time when Japan and China took different paths. The Japanese saw Chinese civilization in a state of decay and turned to the West to learn the secrets of European wealth and power. While recognizing that the West was stronger and better organized, the Chinese chose to learn only what was necessary to defend and reform the distinctive *wenming* that they had. The different roots of the words *wenming* and civilization are interesting.

Civilization in the West described the achievements of civic states that drew inspiration from urban living; the association with commercial and industrial cities has remained its key feature. Here we must acknowledge Japanese skills in finding Chinese words to convey Western meanings. By using *wenming*, they identified the character *wen* 文 as the key to being civilized, the literacy with which the Shang and Zhou states laid the foundations of an enduring civilization. The emphasis on literacy led the Chinese to elevate the achievements of learned men who stressed agrarian family values; the way these men served state and society became central to the idea of civilization.

Modernity today has been deeply influenced by the multiple roles of the city. As cities grew, the mission to civilize accompanied the political and economic expansions of European empires. In contrast, the heritage of a literate agrarian civilization made the Chinese defensive. Civilization was not a mission but more a prized possession, selected parts of which could be reinvigorated with new ideas and institutions. In the modern context, strengthening the state and uniting a Zhonghua nation would provide the basic ingredients for a new Chinese civilization.

Chinese leaders were divided about whether the civilization debate could be separated from efforts to build a new state. For example, Liang Shuming's *The Philosophy of Eastern and Western Cultures* suggested that a holistic approach was necessary. Others too hoped that, inspired by the West, the national state could revitalize tradition. At the other end of the spectrum, younger radicals rejected what they associated with decadent values. If the old civilization could not save China, it should be discarded.

Mao Zedong's campaign to destroy tradition in the name of class struggle derived from that radicalism. The emphasis on the creation of new socialist man assumed that progressive civilization would simply follow when he is in charge. This was why, from 1949 till the early 1980s, there were very few studies about any civilization. Mao Zedong not merely rejected the feudal heritage but also condemned the values introduced by people who were bourgeois and cosmopolitan. By the 1960s, he rejected Soviet ideology in the name of fighting revisionism. He then exercised his unrestrained power to manipulate the superstitions and fears of poorly educated youth. By rejecting successively the Chinese feudal, the American capitalist and the Russian revisionist, very little was left: the worker-peasant-soldier value system that he claimed to be ideal. Words like civilization became irrelevant.

It is interesting how quickly interest was revived during Deng Xiaoping's reforms. Within a few years, a large number of writings were published about building a modern civilization. Debates now centered on looking to the wisdom of ancestral and foreign criteria to start afresh or on constructing a new "socialist spiritual civilization" that would only draw selectively from China's heritage.

They realize that sharing in the global market economy has provided them with new social values and a stronger sense of public responsibility. It has also led party cadres to re-read the Marxist classics to interpret the ideas of popular sovereignty, equality and liberty that are central to the global order and the faith in a moral legitimacy.

It is obvious that new attitudes towards a modern Chinese civilization are forming. One of the important manifestations of this change is to stop seeing civilization as holistic but to recognize that it has many parts and many layers and sectors. For example, political culture is only one aspect of national culture. Urban culture, whether that of the elites or of the working classes, is more varied and impactful than agrarian culture. Professional and entrepreneurial cultures are developing in new and unexpected ways. And clearly, as the country becomes more open to the world outside, a popular culture that appeals to the younger generation is emerging. None of these can remain dominated by a single orthodox political culture as was possible in the past.

Even political culture itself is undergoing change. Ideas of participation are gaining credence and penetrating deeper. This culture rejects the place of hierarchical values in state affairs. Indeed, some kinds of Maoist participation, however misguided, did remove traditional inhibitions. While no one would want these destabilizing actions to become part of the Chinese heritage, there has been a growing distrust of top-down political controls. But it is still too early to say if the wider social forces will be allowed to mature and offer alternative visions of China's future.

In place of participation, there is a culture of management. Here party cadres may be compared to mandarins who knew that if they failed to deliver there would be uprisings and rebellions. This is something no one wants to happen. The managers realize that China must be open if it wants to be safe in a world more open than ever in the past. In a pluralist and globalized world, new generations of Chinese will reach out to many diverse sources of modern culture. They are already freeing themselves from agrarian-based ideas and responding to the popular culture common to industrial and urban societies. A cosmopolitan culture centered in the cities is growing and reflects the demands of new business, professional and working classes. Power elites now recognize that they have to manage these changes while letting them evolve locally in response to new concepts and technologies.

There are at the same time also moves to re-look at China's past. The surge of pride in China's recovery since the 1980s has encouraged a revival of interest in those traditions that can withstand the test of time. This is manifested in new museums, textbooks and magazines, in cultural performances, historical films and television programmes, and in various tourism projects. It is supported by large numbers of philosophers, art and literary scholars, and historians. Increasingly, the efforts to trace the roots of civilization are also linked with calls for morality and progressive ideals.

These draw attention to spiritual needs that require policy changes about religion and the recognition of the limits of dogmatic secularism. If these trends grow, they would challenge the search for ideological orthodoxy that sections of the CCP still hope for. The Party has re-affirmed its commitment to a "socialist spiritual civilization", a resolution passed by the Party Congress in 1986. Although many Chinese might understand the word civilization differently, the commitment to bring modernity to China is firm.

What does this spiritual civilization mean for China today? There had been attempts to introduce some kind of orthodoxy, for example, Sun Yat-sen's Three Principles and later, texts from Marx, Lenin and Stalin, reaching an anti-climax with the *Little Red Book of Mao Zedong Thought*. The idea of a class-based civilization built on a proletarian-peasant-led dictatorship was presented as an official framework in which, as in the past, state power could dictate the shape of a country's civilization.

In China, the civilization was primarily secular and materialist and the Chinese people had no difficulty with that. Now the civilization would be based on scientific socialism. Chinese elites have no real problems here because they accept the supremacy of science and the morality of a fairer distribution of wealth. Deng Xiaoping had worked hard to move people away from slogans and utopianism and return to reason. He advocated a pragmatism that not only drew on past practice but also ideas and institutions from many sources. This mixed approach has left its mark on current debates and also raised questions about the excesses of materialism and the lack of ideals among the people.

From the mid-1980s, this discourse has ranged widely; traditional aphorisms and Western fads have flourished side by side in extraordinary ways. While organized challenges to the party-state's authority are not permitted, the atmosphere is still close to what people have enjoyed for decades. Xi Jinping's anti-corruption campaigns have dampened that environment and state control of academic freedom has tightened, but the China Dream vision promises to open up other possibilities for manifold interactions. It is too early to say what will come from the new rhetoric.

In short, the key debates are focused on formulating principles for China's civilization. What should be at its core? The critical reviews of their thinkers deal with the three main forces that have deeply influenced the modern Chinese mind. The first is to pick out the best of their heritage and anchor the state to those values that people believe to be worth preserving. The second is to be open-minded while critically selecting from the ideas coming from the pluralist world.

The third and most crucial is the view that the CCP favors: that all ideas and values from past and present can be accommodated as long as they are placed in the framework of "socialism with Chinese characteristics". The new leaders have defined these "characteristics" very broadly. They seem to be saying that everything would be acceptable if it can contribute to national progress and if it could help make socialism become widely respected and enable the party to remain in power.

There are signs that the party is widening its options about what can be accommodated as "Chinese characteristics". They derive from traditional values, whether Confucian, Daoist or Buddhist in origin, guiding people's lives even while they are modernizing at the same time. Clearly there need be no contradiction between tradition and modernity. The Party leaders now seem to realize that a narrow orthodoxy that is doctrinaire and rigid could be a greater threat than pluralism. If so, there should be more space for creative habits of mind, whatever encourages the innovations the country needs. The overarching socialist civilization could then resemble the once-dynamic Confucianism that evolved from the Han to the Tang and reached it apogee during the Song.

That may be the optimistic view that stresses the capacity to learn from past mistakes. I recognize it from the writings published in recent years to redefine the Chinese nation. The voice of reason remains respected. Doctrinal hectoring has diminished; for example, even quotations from the Confucian classics are carefully selected unlike the way classical texts were abused in past diatribes. Also, references to thinkers from Europe and the United States are made with awareness of the specific contexts in which their ideas were embedded. More unusually, the pluralism underlying the writings of Marx and other socialist thinkers are now recognized. There is much less that reads like catechism in essays written to make socialism and Marxism more relevant.

There are areas of uncertainty. I shall take two issues in the debates that show that the viability of the new initiatives is yet to be tested. First, the definition of the Zhonghua nation is still open for discussion. Can the socialist umbrella provide the party-state nation with the *civilizational* support that Confucianism gave the emperor-state? Young Chinese are much more attracted by a wide range of scientific and popular global cultures. That variety can provide new inspirations that could challenge what the party-state wants. Secondly, it is not clear that modern Chinese want a state ideology. Enough of them have spent decades freeing themselves from orthodoxy. If they have any say in shaping the future, they are unlikely to choose a state-based set of classical texts. Identifying with the continuities in Chinese history would be more concrete and realistic. The idea of party *dangtianxia* was certainly an effective substitute for the dynastic *jiatianxia*, but the next step towards a *mintianxia* 民天下 citizens-state may be more compelling.

In the meantime, the Chinese people are asked to believe that the nation is the Party and being patriotic and loyal to the nation also means obeying the Party. Given the multi-national base of Zhonghua nation, this may be a necessary stage in China's historical evolution. When the new Chinese civilization becomes more inclusive by representing the wider spectrum of all the most talented, creative and adventurous among them, it would certainly be modern and admirable.

Chapter IV

A System for Progress

The Qin-Han emperors retained the bureaucratic system created by the Legalists but it was the sage Confucius who served as the symbol of successful rule. Chinese nationalists struggled to protect the country's sovereignty and held on to its imperial boundaries but by the 21st century, it was the sage Marx who symbolized the new party-state. For decades, Marx was the man who wrote the Communist Manifesto, while Lenin and Stalin took centre stage. After the Cold War, China found its own way to develop and sought to connect its past with its socialist future. For the marker at one end, Confucius was the clear choice. At the other end, the marker was less obvious but better Marx the scholar-activist with no blood on his hands than two Soviet Russians who terrorized their people.

The first republican officials of the 20th century had to face torrid times trying to understand what had changed and what they needed to do. They had been used to a time when they had hundreds of volumes of *jing*-classics and *shi*-histories together with thousands of edited and raw documents in the archives to guide them. Now there was no republican *jing* or *shi* they could turn to for help. They faced a different order of rules and protocols, a new set of legal codes and the rigmarole of an unrepresentative national assembly. It was not surprising that they clung on to traditional practices as long as they could.

China needed a new political framework within which it could set out its dreams. A mix of nationalist impulses, liberal ideals and capitalist institutions emerged to help the Nationalists establish their regime in Nanjing. The new leaders modernized the administration to conform to the ideas of Sun Yat-sen. At the same time, wherever relevant, some Confucian values were resuscitated. The leaders sought to integrate new and old as the first step towards the delineating principles appropriate for the republic.

I. Marx as Sage

After 1949, "new democracy" was the first step towards realizing the Soviet model. A new social structure was proclaimed in which the proletariat, largely of peasant origins, were the new masters. The photographs of Marx, Engels, Lenin and Stalin were displayed everywhere. Two decades later, when Sino-Soviet relations unravelled, Mao Zedong led the way in continuous revolution and decades of confusion followed.

Deng Xiaoping's "socialism with Chinese characteristics" came to serve as the guiding thought behind his reforms. When he announced this, it would appear that this version of socialism still had appeal. Yet it was not obvious exactly what kind of socialism this was to be — Deng Xiaoping was pragmatic and modest in stressing that China had a lot to do before attaining it. If what followed in the reforms was socialism with Chinese characteristics, it certainly revived interest in socialism. Different labels were used to describe what was happening, most of them combining socialism with some form of market industrialism that was open to employing the best practices of capitalist finance and entrepreneurship. Perhaps it was the Chinese way of doing socialism.

(i) *Away from Ideologies*

Socialist ideas reached China at the end of the 19th century, five decades after the word began to be used in Western Europe. When first attracted to it, Chinese scholars compared them with Chinese teachings about how rulers should care for the welfare of the people and protect the weak from the strong. The comparisons led to radical visions of a communist society that would end imperialism and capitalism in China. The change was akin to saying that socialism had a "soft" humanitarianism image that was shifted to "hard" political revolution. It took place quickly: what happened after the CCP's victory was unexpected and totally bewildering. There was little time for the population to live under socialism as Mao Zedong's struggles with his colleagues turned their world upside down. What then could they make of Deng Xiaoping's attempt to establish a Chinese socialist state?

I encountered something similar when I was still very young. I had gone from Malaya to attend university in Nanjing in 1947 when I heard my fellow students discuss the meaning of socialism. The word had been around for decades and my friends saw it as an appealing set of well-meaning ideals. They could name those in China and abroad who supported political parties with that name. For them, socialist ideals stood on the side of the working classes against exploitative capitalism. They were aware that the Nationalist government was suspicious of its foreign origins so they were careful not to show too much interest.

I did not explore what socialism meant for China at the time. It was enough to know that most of my fellow students saw it as progressive. They seemed most attracted to the idea of a caring state prepared to intervene to bridge the gap between rich and poor and support welfare for the sick and the disabled. Thus the greedy and unscrupulous would be stopped from doing harm to the interests of the country. It sounded so simple that I wondered why not everyone embraced socialism.

Back in colonial Malaya in 1949, I learnt that the Labour Party in Britain represented socialism. The party's activists were anti-empire and sympathetic to the idea that colonies should gain independence. However, they claimed to be quite different from the communists fighting in the Malayan jungle against colonialism. They were against taking up arms to attain their goals. I was also conscious of the ethnic tensions between Chinese and Malays that had been aggravated by the Japanese Occupation, and agreed it was not in the country's interests to resort to violence. In that context, I saw socialism as a progressive part of democracy.

Years afterwards, I learned to distinguish between the many manifestations of socialism around the world. Some democratic socialist states in Western Europe have been hailed as successes. Elsewhere in Asia, Africa and Latin America, many self-proclaimed socialist states failed to deliver on their promises. When the Cold War ended, former Soviet satellite states emerged with modified institutions that could be described as socialist, but none are seen as having anything new to offer.

When China turned away from Maoism and opened up its economy to capitalist methods of industrialization, it was a surprising turnaround. When it espoused socialism with Chinese characteristics, there was scepticism as to what that meant. I encountered surviving Maoists who called what China was doing anything from back alley capitalism to rank opportunism. After 40 years of rapid economic growth, China's leaders feel that the country has achieved something new. I imagine that socialism could always be revised and improved. In China, that story had many dimensions and the initiatives taken by Deng Xiaoping in the 1980s are original. Instead of Chinese characteristics, why not speak of manifestations of neo-socialism?

I am aware that the Chinese have a conservative streak and do not easily call anything new. For example, they would not have chosen "neo" to describe Song and post-Song Confucianism. I recall meeting people steeped in Confucian insights who insisted that it was normal to have the tenets of Confucianism reinterpreted many times. The *Book of History* moved from being rejected doctrine to becoming the core of state Confucianism. Also spectacular was the way some texts reached great heights through *lixu* 理学 scholarship in the 12th century and became compulsory learning for the literati class thereafter.

That development of *lixue* was regarded as the climax of Confucianism. But the Chinese did not call it new and did not use new for any part of Confucianism. It was Western Sinologists who described Song thought as *Neo*-Confucian and identified this body of thought as *new* after more than 1,000 years of disputation. This was done to acknowledge that it was an enriched stage of philosophical development that could be distinguished from all previous interpretations of the Confucian canon.

The idea of newness changed in the 20th century. The generation of Confucians in the 1950s and 1960s spoke of being exponents of *xin ruxue* New Confucianism. The newness refers to contemporary thinkers who were well read in ancient Greek and modern European philosophy and tried to give new meaning to Confucian ideas, further reinterpreting what the Song Confucians had done. Some have improved our understanding of Confucian thought; others have pointed to fundamental differences between Chinese and European ways of thought. In short, *xin ruxue* is new in the way it demonstrated how Confucian ideas could contribute to the study of modern philosophy.

In this context, *new* is different. It is comparable to other uses like *xin wenxue* (New Literature) in the May Fourth movement, and the *xin wenhua yundong* (New Culture Movement) launched by the Nationalist government. In both cases, the newness was linked to the Western influences that had changed what had been there before. New Literature marked a clear distinction between using *baihua* (vernacular Chinese) and *wenyan* (classical Chinese). New Culture was confusing because it often referred to efforts to re-embrace Confucian values. Thus *new* does not necessarily mean something totally different. It may be used to describe attempts to revive something already established and refer to a new manifestation of what has been accepted. The original could be re-examined to see whether it should be thrown out or treated as something still relevant. Where socialism is concerned, the question is whether we know what it can and cannot do and seek to bring forth what is new in its current manifestation.

When socialism came to China, it had been practised in France and England for more than half a century. It represented the thoughtful responses to the economic changes that followed the industrial revolution. It addressed the way capitalists were dictating the lives of the worker. But it was not until Karl Marx published his Communist Manifesto that socialism co-existed with communism and inspired militant movements in France and Germany. Since then, socialism has been modified so often that it has become hard to know what it really means.

At its core, socialism gives an enhanced role to the state and expects the state to deal with the problems created by the capitalist economy.

We have examples of partially socialist states that identified with democracy, democratic socialism or social democracy. These had governments that alternated between socialist and capitalist parties. The word ranges from utopian and liberal socialism to state socialism and communism and its meanings cover a wide span of policies and goals.

(ii) *Focus on Systems*

At a lecture I gave in Copenhagen in 2002, I referred to socialism with Chinese characteristics. Many in the audience questioned how something that has Chinese characteristics could be equated with socialism. During the discussion, it became clear that there were differences of view as to what socialism should really mean. I admitted that I did not know what Deng Xiaoping had in mind and suggested that the traditional role of the state in China could be the best place to start when trying to identify the socialism practised in China today.

This takes me back to when the Chinese literati had their first glimpse of socialism through the eyes of Yan Fu. He was in England when socialism was already well known. He did not call it *shehui zhuyi*, but his translations of the writings of John Stuart Mill and Herbert Spencer showed that he knew that it was a significant movement. He described it with approval using language associated with the traditional responsibilities of the emperor. He associated socialism with rulers who were caring and tried to make a society more equitable, fair and just. Yan Fu was aware that socialists were inspired by the need to check the evils of capitalism. He knew that industrial capitalism in England was not only responsible for economic growth but was also doing harm to the social fabric. In that context, socialism stood for betterment and it was expected that the state should intervene.

The term *shehui zhuyi* came to China from Japan. Literati like Kang Youwei and Liang Qichao had noticed it and their responses were similar to that of Yan Fu. They too saw it representing a moral cause and linked it with the ideal of *datong shehui* (society of great harmony) and other similar ideas in the *Book of Rites* and other Confucian classics. They were also led to think about rulers who were responsive to people's needs and concerned for the welfare of the poor. Zhang Binglin went further to describe *shehui zhuyi* as a body of ideas that provided guidance for wise and effective governance.

The young Mao Zedong had read works by all these men and praised them for understanding that China needed good and strong leaders to create an ideal society. In this context, the Chinese thinkers who first encountered socialism might be said to have stressed the "soft" side of socialism. This was before they learnt about socialist parties that resorted to violence to gain power, in particular, the 1905 Russian Revolution.

On the whole, Confucian literati who had recently been deprived of their privileged social status were unmoved by calls for violence. There were several among them who found socialist ideas attractive but pulled back from the Marxist doctrines that had produced Lenin and the Russian Bolsheviks. They chose to see the softer side of socialism in which its benign ideals could be compared with those transmitted within the Confucian tradition.

There were exceptions, such as Jiang Kanghu and Liu Shifu who were inspired by both socialism and anarchism. Jiang Kanghu went on to establish China's first socialist party in 1911. Both sought to connect socialism with Confucian ideals. Jiang Kanghu even advocated equitable institutions in agrarian societies that the warlord Yan Xishan thought he could introduce in Shanxi province. This idea of benevolent intervention by rulers has been described as "socialistic Confucian".

Yet others who were philosophically inclined tried to probe further into socialist principles. Two who brought these principles into party politics were Zhang Junmai (Carsun Chang) and Zhang Dongsun: they established the National Socialist Party and drew inspiration from European social democracy. Later the two men disagreed as to whether to support the Nationalists or the Communists; their separate political careers showed how impossible it was for socialists to have moderate liberal ideas during that civil war.

The Guomindang emphasis on nationalism and the militarized socialism of the CCP together rendered these supporters of democratic socialism helpless and confused and left no room for their "Third

Force". It is no wonder that, after the communist victory, the only socialism that was allowed was the scientific socialism represented by the Communist Party.

Not all who were attracted by socialist ideals eschewed the use of violence. Sun Yat-sen and his anti-Manchu revolutionaries, already ready to use force because of their secret societies background, were also influenced by anarchism as another way to overthrow the Qing empire-state. Some of them resorted to assassination attempts on senior Qing officials. In his travels around Europe and North America, Sun Yat-sen was drawn to socialist ideals concerning the role of the state. He believed in a state that not only could fend off enemies but also had the mission and capacity to provide for people's livelihood. He admired the ideas in Henry George's *Progress and Poverty* about unfair profits derived from land property and other similar threats to social justice. However, his highest priority was to unify the Chinese nation. In choosing progressive ideas from the republics of France and the US, he concentrated on persuading his compatriots that nationalism was the best way to achieve the country's goals.

Sun Yat-sen never forgot the needs of ordinary people. In his lectures on *sanmin zhuyi*, he elaborated on what he meant by *minsheng* (people's livelihood), his version of socialism. He was not only affirming Chinese traditions of caring and European welfare ideals but also responding to the Russian Revolution that inspired Chen Duxiu to form the Communist Party. By this time, he admitted that Leninist internationalists could help him reunite China. When Sun Yat-sen spoke on people's livelihood, he was persuaded that socialism and communism could be harnessed to serve China. That was why Mao Zedong and CCP thinkers were able to claim their connection with Sun Yat-sen's heritage. They explained that Sun Yat-sen focused more on national unity because the times were different and claimed that they understood what he wanted for China better than men like Chiang Kai-shek who took over the Nationalist Party after his death.

Sun Yat-sen did accept that socialism could be part of the national rejuvenation of China. He was even open to some of the goals of communism. However, he rejected the idea that class struggles were necessary. He insisted that China did not have classes and there was no need for such talk. In broad terms, he thought that the ideals of socialism and communism were compatible with the just and harmonious society of the Chinese tradition. Unfortunately, the war between the Nationalists and the Communists was bitter and long-drawn and eventually squeezed out any discussion about the non-violent features of socialism.

When the Communists came to power, they described socialism as the stage on the way towards communism. Under the umbrella of new democracy, the Party devised transitional arrangements to work with capitalists in Shanghai and other former Treaty Ports. They determined how capitalist ways could be turned into socialistic methods of industrialization and were ready to use capitalist skills to ease the way towards socialism. Mao Zedong, however, was impatient. Thus followed a decade of internal battles within the Party about how fast the transformations should take place and how much the Party and state should be in charge. This led him to challenge key aspects of the Soviet model that the Party had followed and raised fundamental questions about what the communist revolution should be doing for China.

It would be stretching it to call this socialism. Mao Zedong wanted rapid development towards industrialization and decided that the strategies that brought him victory in the battlefield could be employed for the next stage of his revolution. This led him to propose his *gemin zhuyi* that adopted continuous revolution as the speedy way to achieve the Party's goals. Mao Zedong clearly was not content with the gentler road to socialism.

Attention was shifted to an unrelenting class struggle as the driver of change, going beyond what Lenin and Stalin had prescribed. When Mao Zedong launched the Great Leap Forward, he began to use some of the extreme methods that he was later to employ during the Cultural Revolution. His revolutionism made him, especially in the eyes of the young, a bit of a bold romantic but that was misleading. He advocated revolutionism because he believed that it was the only way he could achieve his "imperial" ambitions for China. By all accounts, that was disastrous not only by bringing untold misery to the people but also by damaging the prestige of his Communist Party.

This was a long way from the socialism first introduced to China. It was "hard" socialism that set out to destroy the heritage of Confucian and other social and organizational relationships. In the name of communism, Mao Zedong acted like a god-emperor. At times, he also appealed for sacrifices that would generate national wealth in terms similar to those used by the Nationalists. At other times, he adopted an internationalist outlook and asked the workers of the world to unite against all established authority.

When Stalin talked about socialism in one country with Soviet Russia providing world leadership, he denied it was akin to nationalism. What he meant was that, unless socialist systems succeeded in one country, it could not succeed elsewhere. One country had to show what could be done and, if it became rich and powerful, everybody else would be converted to socialism. It was therefore necessary for socialism to be a success story, perhaps one country at a time. This reminds us that Deng Xiaoping supported the view that some people could get rich first and that would help others. Perhaps Xi Jinping also hopes that when China's socialism succeeds, others would follow the China model. In this context, it is not the ideology that counts but the efficacy of the systems that socialism creates.

(iii) *Chinese Characteristics*

When Deng Xiaoping returned, he pronounced that China was at the primary stage of socialism and will be one with Chinese characteristics. The Party would put aside the previous 30 years of political turmoil and economic hardship and start again with plans that he had drawn up when he was its secretary-general. He argued that the Party had lost its way when Mao Zedong became impatient and took the Party down an unrealistic road. The Great Leap Forward prematurely ended the transition to socialism. Deng Xiaoping returned to the Marxist idea that capitalism was a necessary stage towards achieving socialism but went beyond that to stress its transitional features and its Chinese characteristics. That required its practioners to "feel for the stones when crossing the river". The river analogy suggests that he was not all that sure what was on the other side. The undefined Chinese characteristics were not new. Earlier thinkers from Zhang Zhidong, Yan Fu, Kang Youwei to Sun Yat-sen and others, underlined their view that whatever progress China might make should not be at the expense of its Chinese identity. Although *Zhongguo tese* was not the same as nationalism, it was no less a call for cultural loyalty.

It is likely that most Chinese empathized with what Deng Xiaoping had in mind when he appended the phrase to socialism. They were aware that, after the Cultural Revolution, much of China's past had been distorted if not destroyed. They could understand that the socialist vision inspired by Western ideas and experiences had to be modified in order to succeed in China. The Chinese should not simply imitate what had been achieved elsewhere. The socialist vision would have to be integrated with the Chinese heritage.

Xi Jinping's China inherited the policies that opened the country to the global economy. The policies created the conditions that made China prosperous and, to many, they put China on the world map again. At the same time, what Xi Jinping inherited also includes practices and lapses of discipline that led to corruption on an unprecedented scale. Deng Xiaoping might have expected some leakages in a more open system, but would not have thought that his party cadres could succumb to that extent.

Xi Jinping also inherited programmes from his predecessors "theories" like *sange daibiao* Three Represents and *hexie shehuizhuyi shehui* Harmonious socialist society. Given the pervasive corruption that he found in high places, he must have wondered how useful these theories were. The former was implicitly socialist, stressing productive forces, advanced culture and concern for the interests of the majority. The latter, however, was redolent of Confucian values, made even more explicit when Hu Jintao spoke of *barong bachi* 八荣八耻, "eight honors and eight disgraces". Despite these exhortations, the corruption that accompanied them reminds us of conditions familiar to Chinese dynasties in decline.

If the regime's Chinese characteristics enabled officials to be corrupt and the rich to become excessively rich and selfish, where was the socialism? While no one would claim that everything in China's past was desirable, surely there were better features that could have been chosen to inspire the present. Perhaps not all the corruption should be blamed on old feudal China; the open market economy with its capitalist characteristics is also known for creating the huge gap today between the super rich and the rest. If the capitalist mode is undermining socialist good intentions, are there Chinese characteristics that can protect China from that infection?

Critics have been quick to attack as well as defend Confucian China and the market and no simple answer has been found. What Xi Jinping inherited was a collective leadership system that failed to police the Party. He thus reacted by asserting that the CCP was in grave danger of collapse. The foremost patriotic act was to save the party. He has to find the socialism that could induce his comrades to re-dedicate themselves. He turned to Karl Marx to emphasize its original inspiration and avoided the Russian duo, Lenin and Stalin. By stressing the importance of Marx's worldview and analytical methods, he could ignore the Soviet institutional baggage. Above all, Marx stood for the idea of progress, the modern import from the Enlightenment that has impressed generations of Chinese.

China's modern story began by rebuilding a unified state. Those leaning towards socialism further agreed that the country had to have a strong centralized government, perhaps the most enduring feature of dynastic China. Sun Yat-sen had recognized that and wanted to be the leader with power to get things done. When Chiang Kai-shek seized power, he fought with every weapon available to maintain his supreme position. It was therefore not surprising that Mao Zedong thought that the Party leader should have full control. His victory over the Nationalists had put him in an unassailable position. Thereafter, he could redefine the goals that fit his agenda. He was so successful that socialism in his hands became almost unrecognizable. Deng Xiaoping had a difficult time teaching another generation why socialism was progressive and why infusing it with Chinese characteristics would ensure its legitimacy.

This was the background to the corrupted China that came so unexpectedly into Xi Jinping's hands. From his appointment as Party

Secretary in Shanghai to the Politburo Standing Committee and as Vice-President, he had five years to prepare to become the leader of the country. Some of what went through his mind during that period may be gleaned from his writings when he served in Zhejiang, in the *Zhijiang xinyu* 之江新语 that he published in 2007, but more important was what he thought of a collective leadership that was headless.

Xi Jinping obviously believes that his anti-corruption campaign was vital to enable him to save the Party. His campaign also made him popular and he has tied the campaign to a new faith in socialism. He has emphasized that Deng Xiaoping's reforms saved the state and the Party and are integral to the power that he has inherited. He had worked dutifully in support of reform and this helped him rise to the highest office. His youthful experiences growing up with the peasants of the Northwest taught him about failures as well as successes. That has led him to ask the Party to connect with the first thirty Maoist years as much as study the later years of reform. That way he confirmed the continuity of what he, his father and their comrades had committed their lives to serve.

This attitude towards continuities in Chinese history has always looked to a strong state with powerful leaders. Xi Jinping discovered during his years of service what kind of power would be required to establish the caring and fair society that socialism stood for. When he became President, he not only knew that Mao Zedong as cult leader could not succeed but also that a leaderless collective endangered the Party. He has concluded that the Chinese way of doing socialism would have to be connected to the lessons learnt throughout the Chinese past. Only by recognizing how relevant those lessons are can China confidently go forward to devise the modern state that it wants.

There is some truth in the French saying that the more things change the more things remain the same. The Chinese were even more directly paradoxical. They believed that change was inevitable and hence prepared for changes that could occur several times in a lifetime. When thus prepared, they hoped that each change would not destroy the things that were still valued. If the foundations survived, change could make the new become stronger.

There are other ideas in the tradition that Xi Jinping understands. One is that of *zhi* 知 and *xing* 行 (knowing and acting) and *zhixing heyi* (combining knowledge with action). This had been highlighted since the days of Ming philosopher Wang Yangming. In modern times, Sun Yat-sen advocated *xing erhou zhi* (act then you will know) as preferable to the safer and more conservative *zhi erhou xing* (know before acting) and Xi Jinping seems to share that view. When you act and make your choices, these add up so that you will really know. From that perspective, Mao Zedong's choices taught hard lessons and the Chinese people now know what not to do. Another idea goes back to Confucius, who said *shu er buzuo* 述而不作 transmitting (tradition) and not doing (something new). In other words, without claiming newness or discovery, he transmitted wisdom and knowledge to those who followed. Xi Jinping seems to focus on drawing on past experiences that enable future generations to learn: with learning, something new would result.

Xi Jinping may not need the word "new" for his socialism. His *shehui zhuyi* could be the accumulation of layers of modern experience that harmonize with selected bits of China's history. Explaining the actions and reactions of generations of his predecessors could take his party-state to another level of development. Here a sage Marx symbolically as important as Confucius would add the goal of progress to inherited wisdom. Socialism could be "hard" in rational and disciplined action and "soft" in moral goals deeply rooted in people's aspirations. A strong leader who knew how to link the past to a dream of the future could shape the socialism that his people could identify as the *datong shehui* in China's heritage.

II. A New World of Law

The China Dream is expected to travel on a modern road that the Chinese people would build for themselves. For such a journey, the Chinese had in the past been guided by sacred texts that directed their moral judgments and social practices. And, most of all, the rulers depended on carefully selected groups of scholar-mandarins who were chosen to serve as guardians and interpreters of all state records. So that this was done consistently, they allowed their senior officials to control the selection and training processes.

Today, this responsibility falls on the CCP and its leadership. During his first term as Secretary-General, Xi Jinping found that he almost had to begin afresh to clean up the top ranks in the Party. Since then, he has been unwavering in exhorting all party members to reach for higher standards of competence and incorruptibility. He also observed the failings in the party bureaucratic system in the Soviet Union as well as the experiments by the early republican governments to train modern administrators. There is no shortage of lessons to be learnt and he seems determined that the CCP should connect past governance experiences with the vision the Party now projects.

In revitalizing the CCP, Xi Jinping is not looking to revive the literati of the past or resuscitating their ideals. The Confucian literati and their extended families were the product of a unique examination system used to select worthy men for public office. They emerged as a new kind of non-aristocratic elite during the 11th century at a time when the classics of Neo-Confucianism were being finalised for use to train candidates for public office. At the heart of the education that young Confucians received was to be filial to the family lineage accompanied by the expectation of loyalty to serve the Son of Heaven. The successful candidates and their families then enjoyed extensive privileges.

That literati were a resilient group, conservative in spirit but prepared to be challenged and, if necessary, be redirected. They survived the Mongol Yuan dynasty through the 13th and 14th centuries, became the bulwark of the Ming, and also adapted quickly to another alien rule under the Manchu. During the 19th century, confronted by Western powers coming by sea, their confidence in the broad consensus about what China stood for was badly shaken. Nevertheless, their position was not seriously undermined until the Qing dynasty abolished the examination system in 1905.

In the 20th century, the surviving literati fought hard for another decade to keep their status alive but a determined young generation educated in modern schools finally destroyed the consensus. The new institution of political parties set out to build new ideologies to replace Confucianism. Those who survived joined a new class of "intellectual workers" who adapted to new ways to serve the republican regimes.

Today, these new clusters of workers, whether in public service, universities and research centers or the media, are beginning to agree that a future consensus should be one that has Chinese characteristics, even though they may still disagree as to what exactly those should be. A large body of their writings, embodying ideas and images from multiple sources, demonstrate their attempts to rebuild a consensus. This process is nothing new. It reflects the experience of generations of thinkers who, for centuries after the Han adoption of Confucianism in the first century CBE, thrashed out the contours of a durable orthodoxy.

What is illuminating today is to see how the current debates show that Chinese leaders are responding positively to global developments. Not unlike the earlier three generations of the 20th century, their concerns have revolved around two major themes: what parts of the Chinese heritage can survive in the face of the powerful modernity coming from Europe, and how the national republic can fuse new legal values onto a socialism with Chinese characteristics. As the debates continue under the shadow of serial conflicts, new groups emerged whose education, selection and reward structure remind us of the literati elites of the past but whose duty is to act as guardians of the party-state.

(i) *Recovering Meritocracy*

The desire to save the best parts of China's heritage seems to have resurfaced. Two areas of particular interest are how the meritocracy that worked in Confucian China compared with party meritocracy in a socialist system, and how Chinese elites handled the problems of a society that changed from the centrality of *li* 礼 norms of relationships to a commitment to the rule of law. Both issues will be important as China continues on its own path of modernization. I shall begin with its experiences with meritocracy and then turn to China's efforts to move away from its Legalist codes to learn from a broader jurisprudence framework that is increasingly favored around the world.

The social structure that placed the *shi*-literati 士 scholar-officials above three other categories *nong, gong, shang* 农、工、商 peasants, artisans, merchants rested on the superiority of received wisdom. That belief remained unshaken up to the first decades of the 20th century. The hundreds of scholars who studied Western ideas through Japan continued to search for Chinese roots or analogies for every new institution or development that was introduced into China. The new groups born at the turn of the 20th century, especially those who had also studied in Europe and the US, turned away from cultural concerns to concentrate on building a strong state. The consensus they sought was how to make China prosperous and powerful with modern political methods and institutions.

The people's knowledge base was expanded, especially in the natural sciences that stood out as the secret of Western superiority. Also, there was a systematic questioning of all the values associated with the decadent past. Many literati families struggled to contain the pressure to change by sifting through their heritage for nuggets of wisdom that were still relevant. Their determination that China's civilization should not be destroyed was strong. They hoped that harnessing the best scientific methods to revitalize classical learning and give new meaning to the values contained therein would be the answer. But such people became older and fewer. The young were impatient and forged a negative consensus to discard a failed civilization.

The CCP's victory went further. When its members, mostly peasants and soldiers, took over the state, they displaced former officials who thought they had been chosen more or less on merit. The new criteria were based on revolutionary origins. Everyone whose position had been enhanced by superior lineage, various diplomas, or property ownership was suspect. However, the belief in a consensus remained strong and it became clear that the most common measure of merit was party loyalty supported by familiarity with the communist classics, not least the writings of Mao Zedong.

Party leaders knew that there was nothing inevitable or predetermined about the way the Chinese state evolved. That had included the introduction of foreign influences and each stage of development was always in response to new conditions that tested China's capacity to adapt. The Chinese changed towards the Soviet Union and away from the liberal capitalist West. The forces of globalization demanded greater readiness to adapt. No one, however, foresaw that the fiercest tests would come from within after Mao Zedong had encouraged the Red Guards to go on the rampage. He rejected the idea of meritocracy based on scholarship, and managerial skills were thrown out. When the colleges and universities first reopened, only students of peasant, worker and soldier origins could gain acceptance.

Fortunately, that period of madness was brief. After Deng Xiaoping returned, fresh efforts were made to reassess the heritage. By the 1990s, there was published a veritable flood of essays and books about the importance of historical roots. These extended beyond China and included research on the most esoteric subjects, from the origins of ancient languages, archaeology, religion and literature, to discussions about popular and alternative cultures everywhere in the world.

The interest in modern civilization, in particular, was boundless, recalling the 1920s when young Chinese in large numbers sought to learn about the cultures of the triumphant West. The difference in the 1980s was that the numbers of students were even greater and the speed of transmission of values coming from all over was exhilarating. The thousands of studies published each year since then also raised questions about which cultural values China should cultivate.

Then there was the return to nationalism. As young Chinese abandoned the idea of preserving a Chinese moral order, nationalist sentiments grew in intensity. Whether directed against Western empires or specifically against Japan, this had an immediate appeal for those who saw their country's precipitous fall and felt the loss of self-respect. That was easier to understand than the complexities of an ancient heritage and a civilizational concept like *tianxia*. Therefore, responding to the power and wealth of Western national empires was seen as the answer.

The CCP was in a strong position to build a consensus among its leaders and loyal cadres. The revolutionary elites could draw together a package of integrated ideas through its party-state. They could rebuild its ideology to replace that of the emperor's family-state. They employed indoctrination methods from Soviet Russia if only to teach the doctrines that Mao Zedong thought were suitable. There was broad acceptance that the party-state could end all divisions and a united nation-state would follow. In that spirit, several lesser parties were allowed to remain so that the national project was seen as represented by a grand coalition with the CCP in the lead. That bundle of parties was made to symbolize a democratic consensus.

It was never intended for the parties to act as a *coalition* to reflect a multiplicity of interests. For the CCP, only one kind of consensus was possible. When this was not forthcoming within the Party, Mao Zedong subverted its authority to such an extent that, after his death, it took huge efforts to restore the Party's credibility. Since then, the criteria for legitimacy were based on its ability to deliver on its promises to develop the country economically and achieve the small prosperity *xiaokang* 小康 society that most Chinese wanted. Once again, the party-state began to nurture cadres who could be relied on to act as a modern literati trained to serve the development state.

In the context of industrialization with capitalist methods, what the country needed were people who could make contributions to economic growth. Deng Xiaoping faced two kinds of problems: how to galvanize middle and low-ranking officials to perform and encourage them to take initiatives in their work, and how to select and train a new generation of cadres with professional skills. The most urgent task was to restore health to the country's economy. Thus when the examination system was resumed, the highest priority was given to re-educate the lost generation of young people who had been sent to the countryside and give a kick start to all those whose education had been disrupted.

Here the Party looked to reward practices that were familiar in Chinese history and most people responded quickly. The key was a meritocracy that began with examinations and followed through with continuous performance reviews. The most reliable were criteria used in the science and technology fields and those used by the professional schools. Party membership demanded another set of tests and their promotions were subject to further performance checks. By laying out several levels of selective processes, a party literati community for central government service was being formed. Unlike in the past, the emphasis was less on literary and relational talent and more on specialist technocratic and professional skills and, above all, on accepting party discipline. Also unlike in the emperor-state, the distance between party functionaries and entrepreneurial executives was much smaller. Only in the system of quality control and ideological conformity were there many features comparable to the historic institutions of the Confucian state. The new literati community is likely to evolve quite differently, but if they could become as effective and resilient as the literati-mandarins of the past, their role in state and society could be powerful and enduring.

(ii) *Rule of Law*

This brings me back to the phenomenon of reconnecting the past to the future. During the last years of the Qing dynasty, there was great pressure on China to adopt a constitutional government with laws comparable to those of Western Europe. The officials involved were ordered to revise the Qing legal codes based on the supremacy of *li* 礼 sets of rites and norms so that they could converge with the commitment to the rule of *fa* 法 law. At its simplest, *li* norms derived their justification from hierarchies of relationships, whereas *fa* law placed the stress on equality before the law. This turned out to be a very difficult challenge to core Chinese thinking and practice.

The responsibility to shift the emphasis to law had been accepted early in the 20th century, when law reformers like Shen Jiaben 沈家本 and Wu Tingfang 伍廷芳 met with considerable resistance from their colleagues. For a variety of reasons, even their success in separating the criminal and civil codes was only partial. In particular, the civil code that impacted on deep-rooted social norms pertaining to the extended family proved to be ineffectual. Fortunately, the importance of commercial law was accepted and, for a while, this provided valuable assistance to Chinese entrepreneurs.

But during the half-century under rulers like Chiang Kai-shek and Mao Zedong, little attention was paid to developing the legal institutions further. The Nationalists were bogged down by wars and Mao Zedong was convinced that the laws available only served the feudal and capitalist classes. When Deng Xiaoping began to correct the abuses of power that he had personally experienced, he stressed the need to return to a socialist understanding of the rule of law 法治 *fazhi*. Implicit in his call was the contrast made with the rule of man 人治 *renzhi* associated with the Confucian ideal of governance. Of course, *renzhi* by morally superior Confucians was very different from the *renzhi* that characterized Mao Zedong's *wufa wutian* 无法无天 way of ignoring law and (the will of) Heaven. Deng Xiaping's injunction was to turn away from that *renzhi* and build a new respect for legal institutions *fazhi* 法制.

The question is not new. How far it should be left to moral and upright officials to interpret the scope and relevance of legal codes has been a long-standing issue of governance since the Qin-Han empires. Between the use of *fa* and the emphasis on *li*, arguments have been ongoing for centuries. But, since the Song dynasty, Confucian orthodoxy prevailed and the primacy of *li* was widely accepted. This was indeed the underlying factor in the decades of trade tensions between the British and the Qing mandarins since the late 18th century that culminated in the First Opium War. It led to the imposition of extraterritorial rights for British and other foreign traders on Chinese soil. And it was to get rid of this humiliating condition that the late Qing was forced to replace their law code with new laws suitable for a constitutional government.

Deng Xiaoping discovered that it was very difficult to restore legal institutions that had been distorted or dismissed in the previous decades. Law schools had been abandoned, no formal legal training was offered to people who served as judicial officials and attorneys; people had not been encouraged to turn to the law if they had complaints to make. Most people did not even know what law existed and how to proceed to obtain justice.

All the same, the goal of achieving a society in which there was rule of law was proclaimed while the CCP set out to mend itself and regain credibility. But more urgent matters took precedence. Government organs had to provide opportunities for enterprising people to climb onto the economic development wagon as quickly as they could. In the drive to bring millions of peasants and workers out of poverty and deprivation, it became obvious that a weak legal system was not always a liability but could also be an advantage. When it was possible and acceptable to ignore strict laws and the bureaucratic processes that accompanied them, the result was often to enable businesses to grow more quickly. And once people knew that the judicial system was not efficiently or fairly administered, a culture of doing what one could get away with came to prevail.

What the restored CCP failed to prevent in the frenzy to prosper was the demoralization of the Party itself. The efforts to strengthen the laws and train lawyers and judges were hasty and unsupported by party cadres anxious to succeed under conditions when economic growth was the measure. The remarkable speed at which trade and industry benefitted from the reforms only confirmed that the country had the priorities right. Clearly, the rush to develop the economy could not wait; improving the legal system could take more time.

Most people were aware that corruption among officials and party cadres kept pace with the impressive growth rate. Some party leaders were alarmed but were powerless to stop that from happening. Xi Jinping would have seen enough of it during his years in Fujian and Zhejiang to wonder how long the CCP could survive if that continued. When the chance to be leader was thrust upon him, he re-emphasized the need for the rule of law. This was not much more than wishful thinking when the legal framework was weak and legal officials were suspect. He found that he could only make a difference by using whatever power he could gather to himself and colleagues like Wang Qishan 王岐山 whom he could trust. The paradox for him, however, was that only strong executive power could make it possible for progress towards the rule of law. And if, in the meantime, respect for the legal institutions was not regained, the paradox could swell to become a contradiction.

The history of legal reforms in China has been one of hope and resistance for more than a century. All that time, China has been subject to immense international pressure to adopt rule of law models devised in Europe, Japan and the US. Why has it been so difficult to change when so many leaders have agreed that the rule of law is what China wants? A quick look back at the different premises underlying the concept of law may be useful.

(iii) *Different Heritage*

The distance between the legal systems in China and the West has long been a matter of regret. It began when Britain was no longer prepared to let Chinese law be used to punish British subjects; that issue became the cause célèbre in the Anglo-Chinese wars. Despite the fact that China had, with the help of Anglo-American and other European legal scholars, reformed and modernized its legal system during the past hundred years, the gulf has remained and has continued to fuel an underlying lack of trust. This has once again surfaced in contemporary interstate relations wherever the PRC is involved.

The issue had become sensitive when the Western powers made it clear that their legal ideals were meant to cover the relations between civilized states, and China had been found wanting. The divide stemmed from the European assumption that international law was built on a common Christian heritage. The treaties that followed China's several defeats led to extraterritorial jurisdictions by Western powers and Japan. These humiliated China for being so uncivilized that provisions were necessary for the protection of *civilized* people. The set of practices that diminished China's sovereign rights remained a source of anger for 100 years and colored Chinese attitudes towards all Western reference to the rule of law down to the present.

The different value given by China and the West to the role of law has deep roots. It originated from the different premises made about the relationship between man and nature, between those who moved from believing in many gods to faiths in one God, and those whose worldviews allowed them to live without reference to any god or gods. The single-god world emerged in the Mediterranean region (among

Jewish, Christian or Islamic believers) while the mixed often-godless realm was developed in the Sinic cultural zone in eastern Asia.

When traced far back, what is significant is that, while there were great differences in conceptions, both godly and godless traditions paid respect to the role of law, albeit each in its own way. There was no question of not depending on law for securing order, especially the controls needed for political order. Whether the laws reached into private and family affairs, or were in the main varieties of civil and criminal law, all those in authority gave much thought to formulating them to bring out what was fair and most efficacious. And both European and Chinese rulers paid close attention to laws pertaining to governance, and specifically to their relations with their subjects.

Where their respective heritage parted significantly was the way their rulers institutionalized their codes. Those in Europe believed that the rule of law was a higher principle that stood above other considerations; it was sanctified by the supernatural and therefore sacrosanct. The idea had grown out of customary law observed by tribal organizations as well as in the royal and canon laws promulgated in princely states or kingdoms. In time, they were extended to cover larger political units like nation-states or empires. Law was therefore at the center of all governance and remained steadfast whether the rulers were strong men or a group of oligarchs, or leaders who were democratically chosen. Whoever they were and wherever they came from, they could only rule through regulations and statutes that were seen as parts of God's law. Thereafter, that conception of the rule of law led to questions being asked as to what would best serve those who are equal in the eyes of God. That led people to demand that law should protect people from abusive rulers.

The key point was that, behind the respect for the law was religious doctrine and the Church. In certain contexts, God's law had the power to send even the strongest leaders to the fires of hell. When this authority shifted following the Reformation, Christian Europe still maintained that each church embodied the spirit of God's law. When the classics of the Greco-Roman period were given a new lease of life during the Renaissance, this ancient learning stimulated revolts within the Church. The Protestants reinterpreted their heritage and provided conditions whereby new ideas were allowed to grow. As a result, the advent of scepticism, rationalism and the scientific mind enabled an intense questioning of past assumptions that eventually led to a secular view of the world.

Western Europe largely moved away from church-determined ideas and went on to develop laws that have been described as rational and modern. That saw the beginning of a powerful legal system under which the ruler gave up most of his powers so that his subjects would have more say. Of course, who actually had a say was another matter. It took the British more than 100 years to let ordinary men have the vote, and the women did not get theirs until the 20th century. The British were unapologetic about that pace of development. They thought that the only people who should be allowed to vote were people who owned property and were well-educated. Nevertheless, the principle that people could control their own destiny was confirmed. In one form or another, laws were obeyed in good conscience by god-fearing people and rational scientific-minded people alike. Even when the laws were obviously man-made and could be cruelly implemented, whether by kings, judges or elected legislators, it continued to be understood that a higher spirit rested behind their making. That belief gave the laws a special moral standing and placed the rule of law at the heart of Western political culture. In short, the ruler was always subject to God's law.

In comparison, the Chinese have also long acknowledged that laws should be respected but the idea of the rule of law was only implicitly understood. Everyone was conscious that the laws demanded absolute obeisance; that was akin to fear of the ruler's wrath. Those draconian laws had been given centrality by the state of Qin during the Warring States period. The Legalists who drew them up enabled the Qin to defeat the rival states and use the laws to control, dominate and dictate in every respect. What was understood, and sometimes made explicit, was that the ruler would always employ the law to stay in power.

The idea that rules accompanied by harsh punishments made states strong attracted many of the warring lords from the 5th to the 3rd century BCE. It led them to challenge the Zhou dynasty's claim that good governance came from the model rulers of a legendary Golden Age who embodied the principle that the right to rule had to be defined in moral terms. In that context, legitimacy was confirmed through rituals that demonstrate that the ruler had received the Mandate of Heaven. The rulers of the state of Qin thought otherwise. They employed Legalists who believed that power depended on total control through harsh laws and finally destroyed all rivals to establish a new dynasty. The new emperor made sure everyone knew that he was above the law and his laws must be obeyed.

This law was a revolutionary instrument used to destroy a decrepit *ancien regime*. However, the Legalists were so extreme in their rejection of traditional moral and social norms that people rose in revolt and that enabled the Han dynasty to take over the empire. The Han rulers reformed the emperor-state system and experimented with other ideas. But they retained the body of Qin laws that guided the centralized bureaucracy and brought in non-Legalists to administer the empire. The fourth emperor, Han Wudi, then entrusted men of Confucian learning to balance the harsh laws with their moral ideals. The writings of Confucius had been torched and banned by the Qin. Now his disciples could practise what they preached.

The Han ideal thereafter was to educate rulers in the Confucian Classics that extolled them to be guided by responsible officials chosen for their learning and moral principles. The legal system was no longer upfront but remained there to be used by Confucian scholars whenever necessary. That set the tone of imperial governance even for the Central Asian tribal successors of the Han during the 5th and 6th centuries. By the Tang dynasty, Confucian moral wisdom modified the law codes again, and these were further revised during the Ming-Qing dynasties. In short, laws with deep roots in Confucian *renzhi* provided the foundations of the empire-state for at least 1,500 years.

As outlined earlier, God's law in its secular form came to stand at the heart of the universalism promoted by the West and led by the US and its European allies since the end of World War II. In contrast, the idea of what was civilized in China had been particularistic and the laws guiding its modernization process operate within its own framework.

The country has been prepared to learn from and even adopt Western law codes, but also wants to re-connect with the moral principles that had protected its *fa*-heritage.

This reminds us that law today has not only been a question of adapting modern law for China's use but is also the source of tension in Sino-Western relations. The normative use of law extended by the West to apply to all inter-state relations continues to provide a challenge. Chinese leaders closely observed how those legal institutions have worked in international relations. In particular, they noted how those institutions could not prevent the two wars that destroyed European supremacy. This has led them to believe that the system is not fair or stable and could be improved.

Since 1945, the Chinese saw the rise of superpowers like the United States and the Soviet Union. They saw them less as rival ideologies than as power systems and had tried for decades to decide which of them they should follow. The international organization that the victors constructed after World War II have also been scrutinized. The Chinese look to the United Nations organization as an asset for ensuring peace and want to play an important role in it. They were particularly impressed by its role in enabling the new nations emerging from the decolonization process to participate actively in world affairs.

Nevertheless, the different heritage concerning the rule of law has remained an obstacle to understanding, especially in relations between China and the US. Perhaps now only of historical interest, it was the US that introduced China to the value of international law. The US demonstrated through Henry Wheaton's *Elements of International Law* published in 1836 how law could be used to protect the interests of weaker states. When translated into Chinese, the book taught the Qing Empire the importance of mastering the public law (*gongfa* 公法) doctrines prevailing among the civilized powers.

Although its special position in the UN Security Council has been reassuring, China has not always been secure with international institutions. The US did everything it could to keep the PRC out of the UN and, when that failed, seemed always able to find legal reasons to put China on the defensive. Over the decades, Chinese leaders have been confirmed in their belief that international law was not something universal and sacrosanct that the West had made it out to be, but essentially a political instrument. For them, this was not surprising. They could understand that because the political use of law was in line with China's own heritage.

History had taught the Chinese that law had to be enforceable and only the powerful could enforce international law. That also conforms to their *fazhi* 法治 practice of ruling by law. Where the rule of law depends not on enforcement of decisions made by teams of lawyers and judges but on a sense of justice, fairness and good behavior, it is difficult to see where and when Americans and Chinese could develop the shared legal values that would make that possible.

In short, the series of events after 1945 underlined in Chinese minds the fact that international law was an instrument of power politics and China needed to study it carefully to ensure that its interests were protected. This fitted with China's own understanding of the law as man-made to serve the interests of those who made it. If it is agreed that when conditions change and existing law is out-of-date and unhelpful, then the protagonists could negotiate for its modification or replacement. As for international law governing relationships between equal nation-states, the Chinese leaders could live with it if it was not being used by any hegemonic power to keep China down.

Part Two

Dreaming Beyond

Chapter V

Old World and New Global

The two World Wars of the 20th century brought great disorder to a world that had been dominated by Western Europe for at least two centuries. The victors after 1945 tried to build a new world order with one superpower in the heart of Eurasia and the other on the other side of the Atlantic. When the Soviet Union collapsed and the United States was triumphant, the world order was for the first time in history in the New World. How is China to deal with this new *tianxia*?

China is an ancient civilization of the Afro-Eurasian landmass that shares its five millennia of history with two other civilizations. These were the Mediterranean and the Indic civilizations. All three have developed through mixtures of many cultures in their recorded history. Although they developed far apart on the edges of the landmass, the movements of the peoples residing in the continental heartlands had kept them interconnected. I have discussed the origins of the three continuous civilizations elsewhere. Here I will briefly place all three in the context of globalization in their Old World before the emergence of a new perspective of the Global following the European crossing of the Atlantic. After that, I shall turn to China to look at how it is adjusting to its position in world history today.

The history of what was global in the Old World covers the various efforts by powerful economic and military systems to seek to dominate the world. That global was limited to the parts of Eurasia that transport technology enabled the civilizations to reach one another. Where China was concerned, there are records of ancient trading and migratory contacts with empires ranging from the Persian, Alexandrian and Maurya, including relations between the Roman Empire and Han China. These contacts were primarily by land with some extensions eastwards across the Indian Ocean to the China seas. That was the first stage. The second was when China met Muslim advances into Central Asia in the 7th and 8th centuries. The millennium of expansion had begun with Arab armies conquering North Africa and the Iberian Peninsula and later reaching into Central Asia and threatening Eastern Europe. That Islamic expansion changed the political shape of the Eurasian continent. During this time, their Central Asian converts strengthened the links between the Mediterranean and the Indian Ocean and greatly stimulated China's maritime trade.

The third stage was launched from the other end of Eurasia. The Mongols led by Genghis Khan burst out of Central Asia and threatened to conquer most of the known world. This was a traumatic experience for all those in their way, and particularly for imperial China when the whole country was under Mongol rule for nearly a century.

I. From Old to New Global

In historical records, the idea of the global connecting everyone was not new but was limited to the landmass of what we see as three continents. But, for those living through the first three thousand years of recorded history, there were no continental borders. The Old World developed from literate agrarian societies to urban centers to states established with distinctive political systems. These polities could be cities or kingdoms, but they were all states responsible for different kinds of governance, and the largest among them conquered other states and became empires. Such states normally had well-integrated societies, each with cohesive institutions based on ideals and goals that made it more acceptable to large numbers of people. Those entities that became easier to rule and control could use that source of strength to gain extensive imperial power.

Among those that lasted long and accumulated great wealth, some of these empires developed durable civilizations. The civilizations stemmed from combinations of cultures that together developed systems of ideas and values that made them even more resilient and powerful. Over time, there emerged many civilizations. In the context of the Old World, I shall concentrate on the three that gathered strength on the edges of the Afro-Eurasian landmass and spread their influence over the centuries with the help of the highly mobile peoples at the center of that landmass.

These three civilizations have remained distinctive despite being in contact with one another for millennia: the Mediterranean that arose from the shores that bordered the continents of Asia, Europe and northern Africa; the Indic largely on the Indian sub-continent that spread north and east; and the Sinic formed in the great river plains of north and central China that also spread eastwards and southwards. Each became very powerful and spawned many empires and kingdoms. Together, they were responsible for most of the early historical records in existence.

The people who lived in the vast steppes at the heart of Eurasia were continually in contact with the three civilizations through trade and war. Trade was particularly important for the transmission of values and artifacts, and our historical and archaeological documents provide ample evidence of the exchanges. The civilizations were also connected by sea through the Indian Ocean. The maritime contacts between bearers of the Mediterranean civilization and the Indic and the Sinic peoples were precarious before people understood the monsoons and learnt to use the compass. But, once the contacts became regular, they contributed greatly to the development of all three civilizations.

We have records in numerous languages about the overland contacts of the three civilizations. The peoples in between were known by different tribal names but place-names associated with their activities have been hard to pin down. Modern historians often refer to groups identified by linguistic labels, those who spoke Indo-European, Semitic, Turco-Mongol and Sino-Tibetan languages, with some coming together as tribal confederations from time to time to attack in different directions. As warrior groups, they were the most dynamic, having particular skills with horses that enabled them to dominate their sedentary neighbours now and again.

Thus the three civilizations developed separately but were connected through the peoples overland. As for the maritime peoples, their commercial linkages played similar roles, in many ways just as important. It may be argued that maritime trade was even more vital because it did not lead to destructive wars that were so frequent on the continent.

That Old World began to change after Columbus' crossing of the Atlantic. By the 18th century, powerful navies dominated the world and laid the foundations for the New Global that we have today. Ocean-going navies had appeared in the Indian Ocean before the 15th century. Both the Indic and Sinic civilizations had the capacity but neither felt the need to focus on maritime affairs. Why they did not develop navies is interesting. A likely explanation is that there were no threatening enemies coming by sea, hence there was no need to build great navies. It was enough to have merchant shipping capable of sailing across the ocean's stormy waters. The Persians, Arabs and Indians inhabiting the coasts developed the skills needed to venture out to the open sea while those of Malayo-Polynesian origins expanded their maritime activities to even more distant islands without fear.

Nevertheless, one of the three major civilizations did have an ancient maritime tradition, a very combative one that had been developed to fight naval battles. That was the Mediterranean where the conditions were exceptional, very much in contrast to the Sinic Chinese and the Indians whose enemies came only overland from the Central Asian landmass. For both, these were mainly Indo-European and Turko-Mongol peoples who provided their main enemies for millennia. The Indic and Sinic civilizational core-states spent huge resources defending against overland invasions. India was vulnerable through the Khyber Pass, the Afghanistan-Pakistan corridor, while China was always open to incursions from the steppes and highlands to its north and west.

The Mediterranean, however, was different. There the sea was home to two major culture-zones, one mainly Semitic in origin and the other

Indo-European. They divided control over the Mediterranean Sea from earliest recorded times. The Semitic peoples were primarily located around the river valleys of the Tigris-Euphrates and the Nile, where some built large imperial systems. The Indo-Europeans included those who moved southwards in waves to the Mediterranean coasts. There some of them created small political units, including those based on islands in the Mediterranean, but others established empires in Persia and Central Asia and also built their own Alexandrine and Roman empires.

Both the Semitic and Indo-European peoples had trading colonies yet the Europeans created some exceptional city-states. Although very different in organizational forms, the two types of Mediterranean polities were inseparable: they were continually competing for trading and political advantage and fought one another endlessly. It is significant that the division of the Mediterranean between north and south has lasted down to the present even though political and economic power eventually shifted away from the inner seacoasts towards the Atlantic Ocean. Both the forces were linked up in Central Asia where Indo-European Germanic and Slav tribes fought hard to challenge the power of the region's Turco-Mongol tribal confederations.

Over time, the European and Afro-Asiatic peoples of the Mediterranean found a common faith and converged through a very powerful idea, one that ultimately dominated the whole civilization. That was the idea of there being only one god, or monotheism. Various ancient cultures and civilizations began by having many gods or adopted all kinds of shamanistic and other practices without any reference to god. The idea of a single god came out of Egypt from the Jewish-Semitic peoples. After many tribulations, it led to the rise of Christianity, a religion that spread quickly among non-Jewish peoples.

This eventually overwhelmed the multi-god beliefs of the Greeks and Romans. That provided a powerful mix in which their faith system joined with the monotheistic Semitic god and laid the foundations of modern Mediterranean civilization. Although there were divisions among the faithful about the correct interpretations about god's will on earth, this monotheistic impulse remains powerful to this day.

This was very different from the two civilizations that believed in many gods, or did not refer to god at all. Neither the Indic nor the Sinic was attracted to monotheism. They developed ancient civilizations with their own spiritual values and political systems that resisted several onslaughts and remain distinctive today. For several millennia, all three civilizations were connected across the Afro-Eurasian landmass as well as across the Indian Ocean. That shared history bound the continents together to constitute the Old World.

The Mediterranean, however, saw tense and regular naval warfare. In its mixed groupings of land and sea power, naval battles became unavoidable. One of the most famous was that at Salamis between the Greeks and the Persians, where the battle saved the Athenian states from the imperial system of the Persians. That sea was small enough for small states to train to fight at sea, but also big enough to need navies for a major war. It is extraordinary that we have records of naval battles for 2,000 years of Mediterranean history and almost nothing for other seas and oceans.

The New World was indirectly the product of the naval battles between Christian crusaders and their Muslim rivals. This was an unending civil war between monotheistic Abrahamic religions. The bitter rivalries also involved the Venetians and Genoans and the Ottomans and various Arab-Iranian kingdoms. And, for centuries, the Muslims kept on winning. They dominated the trade between the Mediterranean and the wealthy cities and kingdoms of India and China, including the overland trade where the Turkic peoples were Muslim. And, under the Seljuks and Ottomans, these Turks finally defeated the Byzantine Empire and broke deep into eastern Europe.

On the overland side, the Mongol empires expanded trade in every direction. Their Islamized khanates in the west were inherited by Turks and Iranians while the Mongols who became Buddhists went on to conquer all of China. As Mughals, they followed their co-religionists to occupy most of north and central India. In short, after the Arabs in the 7th century burst out of the deserts into North Africa to the Iberian peninsula, the Muslim powers were by the 15th century in control of most of the world's trading routes on land and sea.

Thus the Europeans found themselves unable to trade directly with China and India. So they turned to the Atlantic. It is not an accident that it was the peripheral Portuguese who led the way south along the African coast. They were far from the action within the Mediterranean and had little choice but turn to the deep wide ocean. The Mediterranean Europeans were desperate to find their way to China and India, and it was the Genoan Christopher Columbus in 1493 who found a new world. With no opposition at sea, they moved from the Atlantic to the Indian Ocean on one side and to the Pacific on the other within three decades. The Portuguese Vasco da Gama was the first to reach India by sea in 1498. Another Portuguese, Ferdinand Magellan, who had earlier travelled to India and the Malay Archipelago, led a Spanish expedition in 1619 across the Pacific Ocean to reach the Philippines and circum-navigate the world. These three decades marked an extraordinary moment in history.

Earlier, the Cholas of South India in the 11th–12th centuries had a powerful navy and the Chinese under Mongol rule in the 13th century had their navies attack across the South and East China Seas. By the 15th century, Ming China had the strongest navy in the world as demonstrated by Zheng He's expeditions to the Indian Ocean. In each case, finding no hostile challengers to their power, neither Indians nor Chinese developed professional standing navies. In China's case, the mandarins actually ordered that their ocean-going ships be destroyed and the empire turned away from naval power altogether. Therefore, there was nothing that stood in the way of the Portuguese, Spanish, Dutch and English ships that ventured into the region. Within a cen-tury, the Indian Ocean was transformed from a history of relatively peaceful trading with local skirmishes into one where naval dominance was the secret of long-term commercial dominance.

The New Global was the product of several centuries of European power in the Eastern seas. The small Portuguese ships arrived off the coasts of India, Persia and Arabia and had won their battles with little difficulty. Their ships then captured the entrepot state of Malacca, took the Spice Islands and reached China without serious challenge. But it needed more that winning a few battles to control the oceans.

The Atlantic Europeans gained access to resources that included natural products and new technologies, and were stimulated by different ideas from the east concerning state, society and cultural values, all of which further inspired the Europeans to improve their own institutions. There followed the advanced scientific methodologies that speeded up the industrial revolution as well as the emerging capitalist economy. By the late 18th century, the naval forces of the British and the French were battle-hardened and no trading flotillas anywhere else could match them. The world thus became the New Global.

II. China in the New Global

When the New Global made its impact felt, the first people to experience it were the Indians, Persians and Arabs. However, through the 16th to the 19th centuries, it was the islands and fragmented polities of the Malay Archipelago that were the most affected by the rivalries among the new European powers. They responded differently to the opportunities and dangers arising out of the encounters and, in general, adapted well to new commercial demands. In contrast, both the Ming and Qing empires were late in their response to the transformative changes that were occurring. The vast majority of their people lived primarily inland. The empires were confident of their continental civilization, had great wealth and rich human resources. Although both showed signs of social and cultural decadence, they were still powerful and saw little reason to be alarmed.

The Chinese officials saw the Portuguese arrive in their armed ships, followed by the Spanish and Dutch and the British, all wanting to trade with China. They knew that these newcomers were different from the earlier merchants, were more demanding and had much better armed ships. But it was not until the 19th century that they began to pay attention, but by that time, it was too late. They then learnt that a small number of British ships could destroy their coastal defences.

The Qing mandarins continued to be slow to respond. For decades after the Opium War, they could not accept that what they were encountering represented a fundamental challenge to their civilization.

They were conscious that they had to learn to fight naval wars against enemies who were defeating them regularly. They had to learn how to master modern science and technology and the financial systems behind industrial capital. However, they saw these primarily as methodologies and did not realize that the ideas underlying them could ultimately challenge the foundations of their civilization.

A few decades later, the imperial system of the Confucian bureaucratic state gave way to the republican forces of the Chinese revolution. Its leader Sun Yat-sen talked about the nation-state model that came from the French and American republics. He believed that the republican ideal was the most progressive available. As for science and entrepreneurial skills, the republic gave high priority to modern education and was quick to build new colleges and universities. Large numbers of students studied in Japan and America and focused on subjects that would enable China to rebuild its economy.

The Chinese also discovered that this globalized modernity offered choices. Britain and the United States had brought liberal capitalism by sea. Yet they could see that the Germans and the Russians of continental Europe had found other roads to modernization. Even the French could offer something different. Most dramatically, the Russian revolution offered egalitarian ideals that were to many young Chinese more attractive than the Western European models.

When the Chinese republic was established, several political parties were in contention, but they were soon reduced to two, the Nationalists and the Communists. The two combined forces to defeat the various local warlords, after which they turned on each other in a bitter civil war that confirmed to the people that the country still settled political successions on the battlefield. Also obvious was that the Nationalists were inspired by the maritime power of the New Global and were ready to fight those who turned inwards and drew on the continental resources of the Old World.

There was nothing predestined about this. Many factors played a role in the choices that the Chinese leaders made. There was, for example, the way the liberal capital system insisted on the extraterritorial rights for foreign businesses and handicapped the Chinese in their efforts to compete. This left the system's supporters with a sense of unfairness. Another factor was how imperial capitalism allowed Japan to benefit at the expense of China at the end of World War I. The Treaty of Versailles assigned Germany's rights in Shandong to Japan; this led to a momentous event in modern Chinese history, the May Fourth Movement. After that, many young Chinese saw the West as cynically betraying their country. This was further compounded when the League of Nations dominated by the victorious empires did not stop the Japanese from turning the Northeast provinces into the puppet state of Manchukuo.

The events from 1919 to 1937 led many to conclude that the liberal capitalist model was not good for China. Whether it was through emotive nationalism or millenarian communism, they looked for alternatives. They had hoped their elites trained in Japan, Europe and America could show them the road to recovery but China continued to be poor and divided and they blamed this on the capitalist system. Everything seemed to point to the need for a different choice. In particular, Japan went on to do what other imperialists had not dared to do, that is, to seize and control Chinese territory by using its modern maritime power.

When large numbers of the young rejected liberal capitalism and turned to the Soviet model, there was nothing predestined about it. They were reacting to powerful enemies slicing up parts of China. However, by making that choice, they accepted the consequences following the victory of the Communist Party. The People's Republic was on the side of the Soviet Union and the Old World. What most of them did not expect was that Mao Zedong would lead the new China that not only repudiated most of China's heritage and defied the United States and its allies in the Cold War but also turned against the Soviet Union that a whole generation of Chinese had been urged to admire.

Deng Xiaoping's opening to the West in 1978 was a clear rejection of the obsessions of the so-called Cultural Revolution, but he never stopped believing in the CCP system. He wanted people to learn as much as possible from the New Global and find new ways to revive the Communist Party and thereby save China. He set aside the ideology that once guided all action; it was the system that he wanted to rebuild.

The reforms were certainly not meant to open up the country to the whole range of Western ideas and values.

What has been done the past 40 years has worked well for China. It has enhanced China's capacity to master all the skills it needs and brought greater confidence in the people's ability to choose what they want to learn from the outside world. In particular, the reforms have enabled the CCP to determine what would strengthen the party and its leadership and what could help a *modern* China find its distinctive character.

One can argue about the rights and wrongs of what China is doing, but it is enlightening to follow the debates since the 1980s on how the Chinese could meet the challenges of the current world order. At one end were those arguing enthusiastically to connect with the American dream while those at the other showed how much they detest what the US stands for. In between were a wide variety of responses calling for a mix of choices that would enhance the qualities of Chinese culture. Reading the debates today, it is not always clear where the Chinese are going. The CCP cadres may be close to agreeing what they still need to learn from the outside world but seem indecisive as to how much of China's heritage should be revived and enhanced.

That heritage is a mixed bag and not just about the Confucian, Daoist and Buddhist practices often equated with agrarian virtues and superstitions. Today it includes lessons learnt from copying the West as well as from the failed experiments of building a communist society. Not least, it also includes building the state led by a very powerful party that controls everything. In short, heritage includes the last 150 years of hopes and disappointments, failures and successes. Having survived those experiences, the Chinese now draw salient lessons from them all.

Xi Jinping seems to give priority to connecting his China with several levels and stages of its past and calls for action to determine which values and ideas might still be valid. In Chinese tradition, change is the norm and life is one of dealing with changes that are unavoidable. That was how their civilization has been enriched in the past three millennia. Chinese leaders understand what happened to China when the New Global replaced the Old and prepare to face the changes ahead and respond quickly when they happen. Furthermore, they have never believed that any world order could be final. It too is subject to change when circumstances undergo change. Therefore, China should look out for what is likely to change and not accept things as they are. When they question any part of the world order, they resent being treated as troublemakers.

The New Global of the 18th and 19th centuries moved west across the North Atlantic and overshadowed Old World Eurasia by the end of the 20th century. The current order was created at the end of World War II; by the end of the Cold War, it changed to look more like an American world order. While China recognizes that the US is the most powerful country in the world, it does not believe that the world order will always depend on US hegemony. Chinese leaders are aware that the US is in an advantageous position by being a continental power with no enemies, a position no great power in recorded history has ever enjoyed. It thus has the power to dominate and intervene everywhere else in the Old World. Hence the belief in its exceptionalism: being free from the warring tragedies of the Old World, there is an innocent faith that, if the Old World could become more like the New, there would be better chances for global peace.

The Chinese are of the Old World and their links on land and at sea have dynamic tensions peculiar to their history. Two thirds of their country's boundaries are continental with the remainder maritime. How can they be sure they are safe from attack? Like most people in the Old World, they have learnt a great deal these past two centuries. With globalization, they now have access to all available knowledge and are confident that they have the capacity to recreate the Old World afresh. They are exploring how they could help in achieving for the future a convergence of the best of the New and Old Worlds. All attainments of the past that are worthy should be reaffirmed. Millennia of our human experience could be enhanced by what New World ideas of progress have to offer. In addition, the debates in China reaffirm the distinctiveness of its civilization and show that its people still want that to be respected.

In that context, those who say that Xi Jinping is calling for Asia for the Asians show their Eurocentric perspective and may be deliberately misrepresenting his views. The Chinese are committed to globalization but ultimately see the Old Eurasian continent as its heart. It is time to recognize that continent's remarkable contributions to the modernization process.

I am not clear if China knows how to make that possible. When Xi Jinping talks about the One Belt One Road Initiative (BRI), he is talking mainly about the Afro-Eurasian landmass and the sea communications along its shores, the world of the Old Global. When China says that the Pacific is big enough, it is affirming the place of the Old World in the globalization process. That is not challenging the US but an assertion of the right to safeguard the country's development and the kind of order the Chinese people need. What they want to ensure is that they will not be dictated to in the name of a "final" world order that all countries must always accept. The Chinese position seems to be that world order must change when the Old World of Asia, Africa and Europe has changed.

III. Southeast Asia: New Region

Perhaps the most remarkable change in China's neighborhood is the new region of Southeast Asia, one that is providing China with a significant test of what a changing world order could mean. The new nations of Southeast Asia have been most directly affected by the shift from the Old World to the New Global after 1600. Today, they are in the frontline of China's maritime initiatives to restore centrality to the Old World.

China's relations with the region can be traced back 2,000 years when the Qin and Han empires reached the coasts of modern central Vietnam. The Nanhai (South China Sea) trade opened China to Indian Ocean merchant shipping and the coastal peoples in between were the active participants in that trade before the 10th century. Chinese ships dominated the trade in the 13th to 15th centuries when Kublai Khan sent the navy to attack Vietnam, Champa and Java. Chinese naval power reached its peak when Zheng He led seven expeditions to the Indian Ocean. After that, however, European traders arrived in increasing numbers and their activities eventually established the New Global system that linked the Indian and Pacific Oceans. As for the thriving Chinese private trade, Ming and Qing official policies imposed tight restrictions that led the merchants to evolve new relationships with the Europeans and settle in the major port-cities.

Southeast Asia emerged as a recognized region during the last years of World War II. The Western allies defeated Japan, the first and only power to control almost the whole region. In that context, the British identified Southeast Asia as a critical zone for the final drive against the Japanese empire. This is also when the islands bordering the Western Pacific changed from being the southeastern corner of the Old World to become the ocean edge of the New World. Since then, scholarship devoted to rediscovering Southeast Asia's past has successfully represented the region as one of strategic importance.

The emergence of Southeast Asia as a region represented a global shift that has been shaping the region's search for identity and a sense of community. This process, however, cannot be understood without going back to the region's fragmented and under-documented past. I offer two approaches to that story. One looks to its history, on the decisions that shaped its polities and cultures when their elites received traders from distant lands, and the other on whether there are commonalities that would strengthen the people's belief in their region.

Historical records of the early states are skimpy before 1600. Most of them deal with the long-distance trade between the Indian Ocean and the China Seas that was also connected to the markets of the Mediterranean World. Architectural and artistic artifacts provide evidence of many riverine states, kingdoms, even empires, that competed for land, labor and trade. Along this maritime Silk Road, thousands of ships carried the trade over the centuries.

The documents about the earliest polities remind us that the Chinese had been interested in these river-states for some 2,000 years. They tell us about the different peoples who settled there and hint at the possible rivalries for advantage by those who wanted to dominate the trade. But with so little on record, we may assume that there were no naval wars or major overland conflicts. Where the Nanhai and the Indian Ocean was concerned, trading conditions would require ships to be armed for protection and key ports being well managed, but not require complex state institutions or monumental buildings.

The maritime coastal states of Southeast Asia tended to be riverine, and their people very mobile. They were mainly the Malayo-Polynesian people, or Austronesian if identified by their languages. They came from South China, in part through Taiwan to the Philippines and Nusantara to Java and beyond, and in part down the coasts of modern Vietnam to the Malay Peninsula and across to Java and Sumatra.

On the mainland, the populations were more complex. The earliest were people broadly grouped by their language affinities, the Austroasiatic languages. The largest group was the Mon-Khmer who could be linguistically grouped with the Vietnamese. They were indigenous as far as we know but were constantly under pressure from more people coming overland from the north down the main river systems. Those who came over several centuries included the ancestors of the Thai from southwest China and the ancestors of the Burman from the Tibeto-Yunnan highlands. The latecomers came down the river valleys and invariably fought for territorial control. We have some records of their wars. The contrast between their fighting on land and the naval conflicts involving the Srivijaya or Majapahit empires was great. The maritime conflicts were never as destructive as those overland.

None of these peoples developed their own writing systems. Their documents and inscriptions used Indian scripts, and the influence of Indian ideas was extensive and deep. In particular, Hinduism and Buddhism inspired the rise of kingly states. In time, the more powerful states wielded power by following Indian models. There has been an ongoing debate about how much the cultural transfers were due to Indian colonists, and how much to local leaders borrowing ideas from India. What is clear is that the maritime peoples spread widely; some went as far as Madagascar across the Indian Ocean and others went the opposite direction to Oceania, New Zealand and Hawaii.

In time, several states were established. We have monumental evidence to add to the literate evidence in Indian scripts, some in Sanskrit, some in Pali and some in local Austronesian languages. The inscriptions that have been found tell a very fragmentary story. Not having a tradition of writing their histories systematically has left a difficult picture to piece together. The states that were created remained shadowy down to the 16th century. It was not until after the coming of the Europeans that more of the local history became clearer.

However, two of the states were exceptional. One in Java produced the great architectural features of Borobodur and Prambanan and hundreds of other smaller structures. Nowhere else in maritime Southeast Asia were there such monuments found. It has been difficult to explain why the island people would build a state with large monuments that could match those in continental states. The other maritime states of the Malay Archipelago were riverine and favored mobility over statist buildings. The classic example was that of Srivijaya as a maritime empire that lasted for centuries but left no monuments. The state moved its capital whenever it was convenient or less dangerous to do so.

The other was Cambodia where multiple groupings of temple-building were followed by the massive cluster at Angkor. Many centuries of Hindu-Buddhist influences may be found there long before the Angkor empire. Challenging the Khmer were the maritime Cham who were equally Hindu; they founded Champa and controlled the central coasts of modern Vietnam for over 1,000 years. There were also people identified by the Chinese as subjects of the kingdom of Funan. It is not clear whether these people were mainly maritime Austronesian or continental Austroasiatic. Some archaeologists argue that they were people of Mon-Khmer origins, but their trading connections with the Roman empire via the Indian Ocean suggest that they were closely linked to the maritime world.

Maritime Champa was not a single kingdom and, despite its relations with Khmer Angkor and the Javanese of the Mataram state, remained a chain of riverine states along the narrow strip of land between the coast north of Hue and south to modern Phan Rang. What mattered was that they each had a port and a river that enabled them to trade inland. Their small states lasted a long while but the

Vietnamese eventually destroyed them. Some Cham stayed on, some fled to Cambodia, while others left for other maritime centers in the archipelago. It was remarkable that the records of the Cham states described Hindu state symbols and institutions. We do not know how these were transmitted. The Cham were quick to build Indian temple structures. Unfortunately many were destroyed during the Vietnam War but enough have survived to show how deeply Hindu they were.

What marked the Cham as maritime people from the Malay world was how they turned to Islam and merged easily with the Muslim peoples of the Malay Peninsula, Sumatra and coastal Java. Those who went to Hainan island established small Muslim communities that still survive. This confirmed that they had always been linked with the maritime world and switched from Hinduism to Islam when their condition changed. They resisted the Sinicized Vietnamese and the Hindu-Buddhist Mon-Khmer and identified with the Muslim trading communities. This suggests how the peoples made their decisions about the maritime-continental divide at key points in their history.

Another people, the Thai who came south to the coast experienced something comparable in reverse. They moved into the territories of the Khmer and the Mon, and established Ayutthaya. This kingdom pushed down the Malay Peninsula and interacted with the Muslim Malays there. The line drawn between the Buddhist and the Islamic parts of the Malay Peninsula remains to this day. Having reached the peninsular coasts, they built a navy to challenge their maritime rivals further south. They sought to become a power that was both maritime and continental but never succeeded. They were constantly under attack from their overland neighbors with the Khmer on the one side and the Mon and the Burman on the other. Facing regular continental threats, they could never pay enough attention to their maritime interests, as evidenced in their failure to prevent the rise of Malacca.

The Malacca story coincided with the seven Zheng He voyages to the Indian Ocean. The maritime empire that the Malacca rulers established bestrode the time when the Chinese would intervene to save Malacca from Thai attack and when the first Europeans arrived in the region. That century of change highlights the difference between the continental Thai who did not pursue their maritime ambitions further and the Portuguese whose fully armed ships pushed as far as they could in every direction. It was a division between land power and maritime mobility that had transformative consequences.

We know more about what the Portuguese did when they reached out to the Red Sea as well as the opposite direction to the Spice Islands. Their ships were lean and fast, better armed and built for war. They represented the bursting out of the Mediterranean into the world's oceans. No maritime force in Asia could stand up against them. All Southeast Asian, Indian and Chinese records commented on their navigational skills. The Chinese were so impressed that they engaged Portuguese to help them build cannons and teach them how to use them to fight at sea.

The Spanish went further. When they took the Philippines, they indicated that they had come to stay as they did in South and Central America. They introduced their religion, their governing institutions and their laws. In that way, one part of Southeast Asia was closely connected to the New Global that had integrated the three oceans. From Acapulco in Mexico, the Manila Galleon sailed across the Pacific to bring Chinese silks and other products, paid for in silver dollars, to be sold as far as the markets of Europe.

The Philippines was part of the Malay-Polynesian world that had not been Hinduized. They had knowledge of Indian ideas and practices but it was Islam that reached the Mindanao coasts and moved into Luzon before the arrival of the Spanish. Unlike the rest of the archipelago connected with India from early times and long open to trade with the Islamic world, these islands were absorbed into the New World. Thus it could be said that the New Global was realized at the extreme eastern edge of Southeast Asia. The people there resisted the Spaniards but were easily overwhelmed.

The maritime world of the Indian Ocean and the China Seas came under Dutch and English control during the 17th century. By that time, the peopling of the Americas and the uplift given to the European economies were proceeding apace. The next two centuries were transformative years for Western Europe: the Reformation, the scientific revolution, the rise of industrial capitalism, followed by the French Enlightenment and the political upheavals of the French Revolution. Together, all these events led to Anglo-French global dominance by the end of the 18th century.

Archipelagic Southeast Asia offered some resistance, but European advances were unstoppable. On the mainland, the continental states kept European power at bay a while longer, in part because Western forces were content with controlling the sea and did not aggressively push inland. This left the Vietnamese, Khmer, Thai and Burmese free from mercantilist challenges until early in the 19th century. Thereafter, British and French imperial ambitions went beyond commercial rivalries. Both had become nation-states with the capacity to establish powerful national empires and fight to take territory wherever they could.

The first great naval battles fought in Asia were those between the British and the French in the Indian Ocean. It is true that the Dutch and the Portuguese had earlier fought in the Straits of Malacca and Singapore. But their battles involved only a few ships at a time, while those between the British and the French were between large naval forces. They were extensions of the naval campaigns fought for centuries in the Mediterranean and the Atlantic. In the Indian Ocean, the French navy challenged that of the British on the high seas and the British won decisively. Thereafter, the British had a free hand to control the Indian coasts and push inland to take the whole of India. The Anglo-French struggles continued in Europe. With the Napoleonic wars and the transformation of all of Europe, the New Global was firmly in place. The land empires established in the Americas were being replicated in Asia and Africa and no part of the globe was safe from the new imperialism.

IV. Global Empire

The maritime world soon became the focus of global power. The British accumulated power from their bases in Madras, Calcutta and Bombay and then, by way of Penang and Singapore, opened up Chinese ports, dominating the coast of China for the next hundred years. The British navy was in full control in all three oceans, with the French navy not far behind. In Asia, the French had to be content with the lesser Indochina and continued to pick up the bits that the British left alone. The Dutch pushed inwards into all the islands left to them by the Anglo-Dutch Treaty of 1824. As for the Spanish, their success in bringing the Philippines across the Pacific prepared the ground for the United States to join the imperialist powers in Asia.

China remained close to the overland Old World during this whole period of regional transformation. Although the Central Asian empires had weakened, Tsarist Russia took advantage of the political vacuum in the vast Eurasian landmass to advance their imperial interests across Asia. The story of Peter the Great reminds us how Russia had hoped to be a European power with its own navy. But locked in the Baltic and Black Seas, it could not get far. In the end, when St Petersburg failed to be a major base for maritime power, its imperial ambitions turned east and south and expanded overland. This was relatively easy because the continental Muslim states were divided and also much weakened because economic developments had moved away from the continent to the three oceans.

The Russians, inspired by the British conquest of India, extended their influence to Xinjiang and Tibet, and to the borders of India, Afghanistan and Persia. With their Cossack forces and a small number of Russian engineers, they quickly controlled large areas of the continent. It was a remarkable story, not so much a reflection of great strength as of the weakness of its land neighbors. However, in global terms, it made little difference because the balance between the maritime and continental had shifted in favor of the maritime. And that would have remained so were it not for the destructive consequences of the two World Wars.

Those two wars demonstrated that the continental and the maritime had brought forth a new kind of deadly rivalry. World War I had multiple causes but the most important was the British refusal to let the Germans project their naval power to their zones of interest. British naval power had become supreme following the industrial revolution.

But when continental powers like France and Germany mastered similar skills and had natural resources of their own, the British felt threatened. When the Germans overcame the French with their unchallenged continental power and turned to the seas, the danger became immediate. The British were determined to end that challenge whatever the price. The phenomenon reminds us of the Thucydides trap, in this case with a continental power pushing its great rival at sea.

British global maritime power was dominant for more than a century. The two World Wars drew the British into wars that they could not win with naval power alone. They could only defend their island advantage against invasion while helping their allies to win the continental battles. This had been true against Napoleon and then the Kaiser and later against Nazi Germany. Fighting continental wars for the British would always be one bridge too far. In both wars, they were rescued by the United States and depended on New World support across the Atlantic. Those interventions showed that the maritime global based on naval power alone was not enough. Without a continental base, the British were insecure. What made the difference for the US was the combination of sea power with total safety on its own continent.

There was, in addition, the unexpected rise of Soviet Russia as a communist state. Russia mastered the technologies of industrial capitalism, not enough to defeat Germany by itself, but significant when given the chance to tie down large parts of the German army. The battle for Stalingrad was a decisive test of Russia's ability to defend itself. By hanging on, it made it easier for the allied forces to attack the Germans from the sea in the Mediterranean and across the English Channel. Even the Russians did not expect that they would, at the end of the war, become the second largest power in the world.

Of the two beneficiaries of World War II, the US was both maritime and continental while the Soviet Union controlled the Eurasian landmass in the Old World. The Cold War reflected the conflict between the open market economy and the continental economies of Stalinist communism. In that struggle, the latter was unable to break free from their land-based limits to fight back at sea.

This was a major factor that made the defeat of the Soviet Union in the Cold War inevitable. By the 1980s, the continental Old World could no longer compete against the capitalist economy. In the arms race, the Soviets faltered. The American strategy to challenge Soviet power economically proved to be correct. With the maritime global under their control, it kept Soviet power in check and ultimately undermined the credibility of the regime.

V. The Nanyang Connection

China remained confident of its own security during these global changes. The events leading to the Opium War had led to some rethinking among the Qing mandarins about the British advances elsewhere in Asia, but there was little sense of danger. For the Chinese merchants of the southern coasts who had been following the expansion of European commercial interests, there were few surprises. For generations, they had been adapting to the changing political and economic landscapes surrounding that trade and had taken every opportunity to extend their activities under the auspices of the colonial authorities in the region. When the mandarins finally realized how much the neighborhood had changed, they discovered that their subjects were well positioned in every port in southern waters.

Chinese in those ports had become wealthy and were influential with local rulers and colonial officials. They not only spoke local and Western languages but were also familiar with the latest technical and business methods employed by modern capitalists. When Hong Kong and the Treaty Ports set out to meet the demand for Chinese labor, large numbers from Guangdong and Fujian provinces went out to join their local-born fellow provincials. By the end of the century, the Qing court had become aware of the value of the growing communities of Chinese living in south of China and in southeast Asia and began to identify them as *Nanyang huaqiao* (*huaqiao* refers to Chinese temporarily living abroad).

From that utilitarian name came a sense of common identity that began to identify with the anti-Manchu movements fermenting on the China coasts. When the nationalists succeeded in establishing a republican state in 1911 the Nanyang label became a badge of pride. Thus the idea of a Chinese nation emerged in a fragmented colonial region where other ethnic groups were equally inspired to seek their own national destinies.

In that context, China and the local authorities saw Nanyang Chinese as significant cross-border actors. That position gave them commercial advantages which different local authorities as well as other foreign mercantile interests found useful. At the same time, the linkages with rising nationalist and anti-imperialist sentiments in China became alarming. Even the Chinese in the region found that the confusion of loyalties often tested their ability to serve different clients and partners.

Until the end of World War II, no one anticipated that Southeast Asia would emerge as a region with strategic potential. The archipelago and the mainland were bits and pieces of other people's empires. Each had become open targets for whoever had the ambition to exercise power and make the people their subjects. Thailand was lucky to be the only polity to avoid that fate. Even the once powerful China was under threat; it escaped colonization largely because of its immense size as a unitary state. None of the European powers thought it wise to try to do more than control its ports. Only some Japanese militarists thought that they could go further. They had observed how the British controlled India. They had also studied how small numbers of Mongols and Manchus were able to conquer the whole of China. With their modern forces modelled on the powerful British and German empires, they thought they were in a strong position to do the same.

The Japanese went further to attack the Western powers in the Nanyo 南洋 (southern ocean, Nanyang). This intervention enabled the shapeless cluster of colonies to experience an unexpected radical change. Japan's defeat led to the beginning of the phenomenon of decolonization. Many of the newly independent peoples — notably the Indonesians, the Burmese and the Vietnamese — had learned from the modern West. The Malay states of the peninsula clearly benefited. The Straits Settlements, and Singapore in particular, was part of an imperial chain of ports linked to the global networks of the British

Empire. This gave Singapore great advantages. But most colonials were dismayed how easily the Japanese overwhelmed the British. Following the American victory in the Pacific, the new nations saw an American world order built on the foundations of the British Empire.

With the world changing rapidly, the decolonization process that gave life to several nations was a totally new experience. The new entity, now recognized as Southeast Asia, was thus offered an identity it never had. Also, former colonies could now assert themselves as nation-states and this made the difference between the maritime and the continental more significant. For one thing, the five continental states had totally different experiences. Most of Burma was part of British India for several decades. Vietnam, freed from its historical tributary relationship with China, was divided into three parts and governed as part of French Indo-China; this had unexpected consequences for the ancient Khmer state and the fragmented units of what is now Laos. In contrast, the Thai kingdom preserved its monarchy and managed to adjust to varying degrees of foreign interventions.

In the Malay Archipelago, there were three divisions that were transformed in diverse ways. I have outlined earlier what brought the Malay states of the peninsula together; now exceptional decolonizing circumstances extended the state of Malaysia to northern Borneo. That brought Malaysia to the borders of the Philippines, the former colonial state in a mixed New World image. Following the US conquest in 1898, the modernizing agenda introduced there made the country very different from the rest of the Malay world.

This takes us to the extraordinary development of the Indonesian Republic out of the Netherlands East Indies. The product of centuries of Dutch intrusions that had begun with a few coastal ports but eventually pushed inland, its territories had never shared any sense of political identity. There was the island of Java with its divided histories, and there were the numerous riverine states connected by trade. After the arrival of the Europeans, Islam spread even further to almost all of Nusantara. A Dutch-educated generation of leaders was inspired by the heroic tales of the Dutch revolt against the Spanish Empire, and by Indian, Japanese and Chinese nationalism, to wrought a new identity in the name of Indonesia.

This remarkable story is still unfolding but promises to make the new country the maritime base of a region about to assume a global role.

Who are the peoples about to shape the new region? There are those on the mainland and those in the archipelago. I noted earlier how some from the Malay world had made decisions to be Hindu or Buddhist and later converted to Islam; others on the mainland turned from Hinduism to Buddhism. One of them, Vietnam, drew inspiration largely from the Sinic civilization of China. In so doing, they all adopted different political institutions and ideals and have held firm to their religious beliefs despite many pressures to change. They now each have a distinctive role to play in determining the quality of the region's identity.

In maritime Southeast Asia, the experiences have been strikingly different. The peoples there are more open to what they have inherited from the colonial states. They have found that heritage workable. They have sought to localize and improve what they have retained and turn that heritage into something that their people can identify with. They recognize the heritage as new and malleable, as can be seen in the practical ways they responded to the Cold War. The example of state formation that created the states of Malaysia and Singapore is exemplar of this pragmatism. The violent removal of President Sukarno and the radical shifts in economic policies by President Suharto turned out to be restorative to the Indonesian state. These were very different decisions that transformed each country; they were choices made to enable the countries build new nations out of the colonial systems they inherited.

Here I highlight a decision that the maritime peoples made that would not have been possible had it been left to those on the mainland. It was a fine example of the pragmatism that the region is capable of practising. I refer to their coming together to form the Association of Southeast Asian States (ASEAN) in 1967. Five nations, with Thailand primarily on the mainland, did this in the middle of the Cold War when countries were forced to choose whether to stand with the capitalists or with the communists. The establishment of ASEAN divided the region between those that supported the Americans in the Vietnam

War and those who would have preferred not to have the war at all. With its affinity with the New Global, the archipelagic world's choice to be associated with the Anglo-American world order was not surprising.

After World War II, the new world order was consolidated by the US victory over the Soviet Union in the 1990s. This is essentially an ocean-based order rooted in 200 years of the New Global that is also backed by the continental security of North America. One major beneficiary of this order was China opened up by Deng Xiaoping's reforms. His policies opened China to the global market economy and confirmed that secure maritime transport was the key to China's recovery. The success of the policies has made China more conscious that it must have the capacity to protect their interests at sea. By the 1990s, the Chinese had turned their full attention to shipbuilding and naval training.

The Chinese are now committed to naval development, a policy that clearly concerns their maritime neighbors. At the same time, they have not forgotten that their continental borders are long and insecure. It is also vital that they manage their overland relations well. The US knows that its leadership in the New Order comes from having over-whelming naval power and not being fearful of overland threats. The Chinese are not that fortunate. While trying to secure their maritime linkages, especially in their own neighborhood, they must remain ready to protect their land frontiers. They recognize that a comprehensive Eurasian strategy to win friends in the Old World is essential for long-term safety.

Today a new Southeast Asia can work through ASEAN. This regional organization is a remarkable achievement, but it is still work in progress. Beginning with maritime interests, it now includes continental states with very different histories. Vietnam, for example, learnt the same lessons as the Chinese and now looks much more to the sea while Laos is totally landlocked. As for Cambodia and Myanmar, how they respond to maritime challenges is still unclear. As members of ASEAN, this may matter less as long as they can count on a united organization to monitor the region's naval concerns.

Here ASEAN's efforts could make it greater than its parts. The region's location between the Indian and Pacific Oceans ensures that the great maritime powers of the world will always have a strategic interest in its wellbeing. But there are analogies with the Mediterranean world that may be relevant. Although on a smaller scale, naval power in that sea determined the fates of all the states involved, deep divisions between the states on its northern and southern coasts have lasted to this day. It is never a question of naval power alone. The states facing the sea have strong hinterlands and neither those of the north nor of the south could dominate the Mediterranean for long. That should remind us that Southeast Asia with its continental and maritime members could also be vulnerable to divisions when confronted by external forces coming from different directions and calling on each of its member states to choose sides.

Another interesting question is why the South China Sea was never a zone of naval conflict the way the Mediterranean was. It is narrower in parts and wider in others and not well sealed like having Gibraltar at one end and Suez at the other. There are more openings to the ocean, as in the Taiwan Strait, the Sunda and Malacca Straits, as well as the passages leading into the South Pacific. In addition, unlike the Mediterranean where there were always powerful states on both sides of the sea, there was no power that could challenge the Chinese empire in the South China Sea. Had there been one, perhaps that sea would also have been a zone of tense and extended competition from ancient times.

That may be about to change. Today, the newly announced Indo-Pacific front has created a counter-power to face a rising China. At the same time, dynamic economic growth is moving from the Atlantic to this extended maritime space. Together, they have given new life to the Old World. Thus countries like China and India are building more credible navies to match those of Japan and the United States. In that way, the Indo-Pacific could serve as a larger Mediterranean in which the South China Sea acts as its strategic center. That would make the double-ocean zone one of continuous tension in which powerful protagonists will keep the divisions permanent.

If ASEAN is divided underneath that overarching framework, it would be of little use to anybody. The region's history renders it open to divisions, especially between the mainland and the archipelagic states that tend to look in different directions for their wellbeing. However, if these states can overcome their historical baggage, ASEAN could have a major role to play in the midst of the rapid changes in the relations between the New Global and Old World. If it is united on critical issues, it could provide a bridge that helps to make those relationships peaceful and constructive. That would not only help its members withstand the pressures put on them, but also demonstrate to all major powers that their interests are also best served by a truly united ASEAN.

Chapter VI

China's South

The previous chapter outlined the changes in the world order during the past century that China had to overcome after the most damaging fall in its history. The chapter also highlighted the role of Southeast Asia in that fall and the way the region has grown in importance now that the world order is once again being restructured. China's future will depend more than ever on how it manages its coastal lands and its southern neighbors. In this final chapter, I trace the shifting perspectives of north and south in Chinese history and describe the circumstances that created the divergences experienced by the country's rulers and elites. The first Chinese emerged in the north but large numbers of them moved south over two millennia; significantly, many continued to seek legitimacy through northern cultural sites. However, settling in the south had always been deeply enriching and, despite political and military power remaining in the north, it was the south that had adapted more readily to new challenges.

In my introduction on "Studying China", I briefly mention the turning points in my efforts to learn about China. I grew up with the idea of oneness in the Chinese heritage but was soon made aware of the gap between the people in the south who traded in the Nanhai and the militarist empire-builders of northern China. When I was teaching early modern history and comparable features of Chinese and Mediterranean historiography, I also learnt to see China's ambivalence about continental and maritime power. By the time I came to study the People's Republic of China's efforts to reposition itself in the new world order, I could see how China's south has become more important than it has ever been before.

When I began my first and only course on Chinese history as an undergraduate, I thought everybody knew where China was, and saw the 5,000 years of history of China as straightforward. At the National Central University in Nanjing in 1947, one of the compulsory subjects for first-year students was General History of China. The three volumes by Miao Fenglin covered some 5,000 years down to the 20th century. I also read another three volumes of the Cultural History of China by Liu Yizheng. They were both leading historians of the time and I assumed that reading these two books was more than enough. Years later, in Singapore and London, I remedied that by reading the works of several other historians, notably Qian Mu, Chen Yinke, Gu Jiegang, Fu Sinian, Zhou Yiliang and a number of Marxist historians like Lu Zhenyu, Fan Wenlan and Jian Bozan. By then, I could see how many Chinas there were and how far away I was from understanding its history.

Literature had been my first love and I did not expect to be a historian, so it was years later before I realized how wrong I was. After my first year, the civil war was going badly for the Kuomintang and the People's Liberation Army reached the north banks of the Yangtze River. In November 1948, the university was disbanded and I went back to Malaya. I then studied at the new University of Malaya in Singapore where, for the three-year BA degree, we did three subjects. I chose English literature and economics. For the third subject, I did not want to take geography and thought that history would be more interesting.

At the end of my third year, I chose to read history for my Honors degree. In my first three years, I studied modern history about Europe in Asia: the rise of Western empires with Asia peripheral to what the Europeans were doing. It was an absorbing story at a time when getting rid of the imperialists had become part of our daily conversations. I had never liked the British and Commonwealth history taught in school, but university history was different. I found to my surprise that Europe's role in the decline and fall of Asia was very interesting.

Our professor, C.N. Parkinson, taught us to use primary sources in the archival collection at the Raffles Library. I looked for a topic that was linked to some aspect of modern Chinese history and saw that Sun Yat-sen and Kang Youwei and their supporters had been active in Southeast Asia. Both had stayed briefly in Singapore and Penang before moving elsewhere. Their lives were remarkable and I took the opportunity to learn about the story of China's early efforts at modernization. Professor Parkinson helped me to go to Hong Kong to search for more documents and interview early reformers and revolutionaries who were still alive. The work was exciting and I decided to continue studying history.

For my Master's degree by research, I was disappointed to find that I could not continue with modern Chinese history. Anything about modern China was suspect at a time when British troops in Malaya were fighting a communist insurgency led by local Chinese. Books published on the Chinese mainland were restricted and there was no question of access to Chinese archives. If I wanted to do research on China, it would have to be something pre-modern. So I chose to study how Chinese first traded in the Nanhai, the South China Sea.

My earlier work on Sun Yat-sen and Kang Youwei, both Cantonese from the Pearl River delta, had made me aware that there were several million Chinese living in Southeast Asia and that they came from the provinces of Guangdong and Fujian with different backgrounds from my own. My parents came from Jiangsu and my father's family had migrated south from Hebei during the 19th century and, in Jiangsu, they were treated as sojourners from the north. Our family did not speak any southern dialect but one closer to modern *putonghua*. Growing up in Malaya, I did learn some of the dialects spoken, but was aware that South China was different from the China my parents talked about. The classical texts that my father taught me to read were focused on famous writers and poets from northern China and hardly ever mentioned the south. Nevertheless, I had no doubt that we were Chinese who shared the same history.

In London for graduate research, I first wanted to study early Ming relations with Southeast Asia but the professor I had hoped to study with was leaving. So I spent my first year there looking for another subject. I had been curious about the numerous warlords who had carved up the Republic of China and why it was so difficult to reunify the country. But, with no access to Chinese archives, I could only study an earlier period of military fragmentation that would help me to understand. This led me to the Five Dynasties and Ten Kingdoms period that followed the fall of the Tang dynasty, one of the most divisive periods in Chinese history.

I began by reading about the southern kingdoms: Southern Han 南汉 in Guangdong, Min 闽 in Fujian, Wu Yue 吴越 in Zhejiang and Nan Tang 南唐 in Jiangsu, and was intrigued by the way they had to fight to survive and that, finally, it was the Song emperors in the north that united the country. This encouraged me to focus on the northern Five Dynasties to discover how this happened. After all, the classics of literature projected an image of China as the world of the Yellow River where core ideas and values had emerged from the intense interactions between the plains of Hebei, Henan and Shandong and the uplands of Shanxi and Shaanxi, the cradle zones of Chinese civilization. There was very little about the south.

I. From the North

I began to see the way northerners perceived China's south and how people in the south related to the Chinese state. Where did the differences come from? Why does it matter? These were questions that surfaced when I did my North China research. When I returned to Malaya in 1957, I taught Ming and Qing history from the 15th century to the Opium War. The period was one when China was the dominant power in East and Southeast Asia but then rapidly declined. By teaching the course for 10 years, I better understood the trajectories of dynastic decline and fall and why that phenomenon dominated the narratives of north and south in different ways.

Turning to how the north perceived China's south from early times, there were at least three *souths* — the southeast; the southwest; and a further south that both were linked to. Most of the south were peopled by what northerners called the "Hundred Yue", *Baiyue* 百越 or "Southern Man" *Nan Man* 南蛮. Those of the southwest were separately described as "Southwest Man" *Xinan Man* 西南蛮. There was no single name for peoples further south but they included more distant peoples who came to trade at the riverine ports of Yue territory as well as the upland towns of the southwest.

When the Qin and Han rulers consolidated their control over the southern lands that they conquered, the lands of the *Baiyue* became part of the Chinese empire. Over the next millennium, these lands attracted large numbers of settlers from the north. In the southwest, other Chinese settlers did move to the uplands, but the imperial authority decided to leave most of the *Xinan Man* alone. The most important changes came about during the 4th century. That was when the "five Hu (tribes) overwhelmed the (Chinese) Hua" *Wuhu luanhua* 五胡乱华. The invaders were the ancestors of peoples later known as Turkic, Tibetan, Mongol and Jurchen-Manchu; they established their 16 kingdoms and brought Han China to an end.

Their invasions led to a series of northern dynasties being established through collaborations between the Hu and Han peoples. The Han Chinese who refused to collaborate moved south, across the Yangtze River to Zhejiang and Fujian, the southern valleys of Jiangxi and Hunan, and across the mountains to the *Lingnan* 岭南 areas. These migrations, comparable to refugees, consisted largely of families with retinues of servants and retainers and were well armed to defend themselves in the southern wilds.

Thus a new and smaller "China" was established under a succession of four Southern Kingdoms, the Song, Qi, Liang and Chen dynasties 宋齐梁陈. In the north, however, the Turkic Tuoba 拓跋 who founded the northern Wei 魏 dynasty took control and it was their Sinicized descendants of the Sui and Tang dynasties that brought "south China" back into the fold. By that time, the economy of the Yangtze delta region was highly developed and the empire's growth centers shifted southwards from the plains of the Yellow River. With growing wealth and cultural confidence, the Tang people *Tangren* 唐人 in the south could boast that they were more authentically Chinese than the northerners.

Historians sometimes ask whether the less than Chinese northerners are more Chinese than the southerners who were not fully Chinese. What is significant is that both northerners and southerners had become Chinese at different times and in different ways. When I studied the Five Dynasties period, I was surprised to learn how much the northern *five* dynasties were unlike those kingdoms that were established in the south.

The other question that interested me was how such a divided China could become one again. The Song 宋 dynasty almost reunited all of China as the *sixth* dynasty after the "Five Dynasties" in the north; it was also one led by a mixture of Chinese and Tuoba military leaders. However, the Song emperors failed to retake the 16 prefectures that had become part of the Khitan Liao empire, including the areas around modern Beijing. As a result, they were largely on the defensive for the next two and a half centuries, continually under pressure by non-Han forces like the Khitan Liao, the Jurchen Jin and the Tangut Western Xia.

After defeat by the Jurchen Jin, the Song was forced to move its capital to Hangzhou. There its emperors were in effect southerners who had to concentrate on building an independent Song Kingdom *Song Guo* 宋国. This meant building a kingdom under the cover of an ideal All under Heaven *tianxia* that its scholar-mandarins had to redefine. They did so by reinterpreting the Confucian Classics, drawing on the wisdom of Buddhist and Daoist thinkers and practitioners while doing so. They also used the experiences of generations of Confucian officials who had served both northern and southern dynasties since the fall of the Han. Thus a revitalized body of Confucian thought was gathered together to become the new orthodoxy, *Lixue* 理学 Neo-Confucianism. In this way, China's south could claim to be the China that saved the core values of civilization.

This success story was based on the talents of enterprising southerners who developed the economic potential of coastal resources combined with those of elite migrants who had brought their cultural authority with them when the Song was forced southwards. The Neo-Confucian canon that emerged was the product of two centuries of revisions and renewals during times of desperate defence. In the end, this was the gift from the south to the north when China was reunified, first by the Mongol Yuan followed by the Ming and Qing. The paradox here comes from the fact that the separation from the north had enabled the south to gain its own authoritative voice; this gave the southern literati the right to shape the future China when they were given the opportunity to do so.

The next political change in Chinese history came from outside China because the Song Chinese had failed to put a broken China back together again. When the Mongols finally defeated the Western Xia and the Jurchen Jin, that opened the door for Kublai Khan to conquer the Song kingdom. The whole of China was once again unified, something that no ruler had been able to do since the 9th century. For China's south, the Mongol conquest was a transformative moment. For the first time in history, *all* of China was ruled not by northern Chinese but by northern *non*-Chinese.

The Mongols were brutal and destructive conquerors. They devastated most of the lands they conquered for a period of 70 years before defeating the Song. Their ambition to rule the world did not stop at the land edges; from the China coasts, they even set out to conquer countries across the seas. However, Kublai Khan did adopt Chinese ideas of legitimacy by seeing the Yuan dynasty as the successor of the Liao and Jin dynasties as well as the Song. He not only kept all of China together but also, 92 years later, his successors left a united China for Zhu Yuanzhang, a southerner from Anhui, to inherit and rebuild as a Han-Chinese Ming dynasty.

I call this a transformation because the reintegration of China's south was a total success. Another 300 years later, the Manchu Qing from outside the Great Wall also conquered all of China. As descendants of the Jurchen Jin, they claimed to know how China should be governed. But, unlike the Mongols, they were a tribal confederation from the forests of Manchuria and were helped by having the Mongols as partners when they marched into China. Later, the Qing pushed further north and west and, like the Mongol Yuan, created a larger "China" that looked beyond traditional borders across to the Eurasian landmass. They conquered Xinjiang-Turkestan, dominated the Tibetans, and redrew the map of what has come to be recognized as the historic China.

The Qing imperial map reminds us that China has never been a country, kingdom or empire of fixed and unchanging borders. For example, if the Qin and Han, the Sui and Tang, the Song, Yuan, Ming and Qing can all be called Chinese dynasties, every one of them had a different set of borders. Not being a Han-Chinese dynasty, the Mongol Yuan and the Manchu Qing were not inhibited by Chinese traditions of what *tianxia* referred to. They used the economic resources of China to support their expansions and administered Han-Chinese territories the way they thought appropriate. As for the lands that had never been part of China, they drew up new boundaries and managed them quite separately. In that way, the Mongol conquest made questions of what was north and what was south within a unified China increasingly complex. What endured was the reintegration of north and south China and the recognition that the south had laid the foundations of a new imperial orthodoxy.

There was another change to the map of China, this time in the south, that turned out to be equally enduring. The Mongols had marched south from Gansu and western Sichuan into Yunnan and incorporated into their empire most of the lands of the southwest *Xinan Man*, that is, southern Sichuan, Yunnan, Guizhou and western parts of Guangxi. For centuries, those areas had their own independent states, notably the Nanzhao and Dali kingdoms. But the Mongols did something that no other conqueror of China had ever tried. They invaded China not only frontally across the Yellow and Yangtze rivers but also from the southwest and, in a two-pronged attack, destroyed the Southern Song. There followed a long process of integration of this "new southwest" under the Ming, and the system of *tusi* 土司 administration by local chieftains was systematically dismantled during the Qing dynasty. What remains of that system today are the autonomous towns and prefectures reserved for various minority peoples or "nationalities" that are controlled by central officials appointed to provincial governments.

The process of reintegration by the Mongols from their capital in Beijing had been tentative; the Ming emperors completed the task after they drove the Mongols out. The founder first moved the capital south to Nanjing to affirm the new orientation but Zhu Di, Emperor Yongle, usurped the throne after his father's death and moved the capital back to Beijing. He was the first Han Chinese emperor to rule China from that city and, from that time on, the center of political power has mainly remained in the north. Beijing today is largely the city that Yongle had mapped and built.

The significance of this move was profound. It originated from the time when Zhu Di was enfeoffed as Prince of Yan 燕王 and made leader of the forces in Beijing to defend key parts of the northern frontier. For at least 30 years, he faced endless Mongol attacks and was widely respected as a dynamic military leader. From the old Yuan palaces in Beijing, he was alert to the ambitions of Timur and the Mongol-Turk armies that sought to dominate central and western Asia. And, while his father had revived traditional Chinese ideas of *tianxia* and called for the restoration of Han and Tang glory, he had developed a more extended and inclusive worldview. When he became emperor and decided to return the capital to Beijing, he saw that this would allow him to reclaim what might be called a Mongol-influenced idea of *tianxia*, a worldview that emanated from Beijing. One of his reactions against Timurid expansions in Eurasia, sending Zheng He's naval expeditions to the Indian Ocean, point to that larger perspective.

Under the Mongol Yuan, the Chinese of the conquered Song were designated the "southern people" *Nanren* 南人, the fourth and lowest tier of the Yuan population. With an all-powerful center lodged in the north, the *Nanren* literati had to review their position as a forsaken elite group. As they pondered their future, they continued to see themselves as bearers of the Confucian wisdom that had flowered during the Song. They carefully conserved that image while successive Mongol rulers turned to Daoists and Buddhists for spiritual guidance. Their reorientation under rulers who were by and large indifferent to their skills enabled them to keep their self-respect and eventually won them the right to restore parts of the Song examination system during the later period of the Yuan.

Their perseverance was finally rewarded when the Ming emperors set out to restore Chinese moral and political values. As torchbearers of the Neo-Confucian heritage, the southern literati were brought back to the central offices. This included being entrusted to tutor the imperial household and conduct all the examinations for public office. Southern examination graduates held high offices and could stand up to the reduced northern elites. The heritage sites might be located in the north but, to these literati, it was their southern minds that had climbed the steep slopes of timeless wisdom. That made them proud to say that China's south was the true home of an impeccable Neo-Confucian civilization.

II. The South Looks Back

There are no records of what the southern Yue people thought of "the Chinese" before they came south to settle. The little we know about their early contacts came from the impressions left by northerners who served as officials or were sent south as exiles. Some wrote poems and essays about people who were not at all like themselves. Over the centuries, the various peoples lived together and those who identified as *Tangren* developed local customs and lifestyles. Only the educated elites still conformed as much as they could to the northern cultural traits that their ancestors had brought with them, notably those transmitted through literary works, Confucian classics and some Buddhist and Daoist texts.

It was significant that the southerners adapted to living in terrains quite different from those in the north. Most of them settled in the valleys of smaller rivers that flowed into the East China and South China Seas and were separated by hill ranges. As riverine peoples living in these valleys, they evolved different kinds of agrarian communities. Those closer to the river mouths developed trading centers, some of which were large enough for them to establish local kingdoms with distinctive cultures. The best example south of the Yangtze delta was the much smaller river Qiantang jiang 钱塘江 in the ancient kingdom of Yue, later the basis of Wu Yue kingdom in the 10th century and provided the capital of the Southern Song. Further south were others that played similar roles: the Minjiang that was home to the ancient Min Yue 闽越 and later, in the 10th century, the kingdom of Min. And then small rivers like the Jiulong jiang 九龙江 of Zhangzhou and in the Hanjiang 韩江 of Chaozhou, whose Min-dialect speakers established their own ports and shipping centers that produced some of the most adventurous traders of the East and South China Seas.

To their west, the rivers have a different orientation and became the center of a larger political unit that was no less riverine. That was the famous kingdom of Nan Yue 南越 that had its capital in Guangzhou. The powerful kingdom was developed bestriding the valleys of the West River Xijiang and East River Dongjiang where the two rivers met at the delta now known as the Pearl River Zhujiang. Here was rich agricultural land comparable in some ways to those of the Yangtze delta, although the two rivers are not as spectacular. The Nan Yue kingdom did produce a rich culture of its own but it was not strong enough to withstand the onslaughts by the forces of the Qin-Han empires. In the end, in contrast to the extensive northern plains that determined the shape of imperial China, the Nan Yue was more like a riverine state.

Further west was another riverine state contemporary with the Nan Yue. This was the Luo Yue 骆越 kingdom that developed its distinctive cultural center along the Red River Honghe in northern Vietnam. That kingdom was equally dominated by the Qin-Han empires and also subject to northern Chinese influences over several centuries. But fewer Chinese migrated that far south and, after the Tang dynasty, the chiefs of the Vietnamese peoples were able to make use of some powerful Chinese institutions to set up their own independent kingdom.

These ancient southern kingdoms became sites for sizeable riverine states but they could not muster any combined power to challenge forces sent from the north and never had the capacity to take over the whole of China. The military superiority of the north was derived from the need to share resources on a very large scale to deal with problems associated with great rivers liable to flood and open plains difficult to defend. Northerners had to learn how to handle the distribution of power in those areas that they managed to hold and control. It required these Chinese to fight endlessly in large numbers, thereby helping them to be militarily well organized and powerful.

In the southern riverine systems, most communities were content to be separate and distinct. In many ways, large parts of southern China have similar riverine conditions as the mainland parts of Southeast Asia. There, too, port cities close to the mouths of rivers tended to be developed as polities that became the capitals of kingdoms and even compact little empires. The best examples close to China's frontiers were the small port towns along the coast of what today is central Vietnam where small rivers flowed into the South China Sea. These trading centers cooperated and functioned as a distinct polity known to the Chinese first as Linyi 林邑 and later identified as Champa or Zhancheng 占城 but they could not establish an enduring and powerful kingdom. Similarly, the maritime trading polity to their west known as Funan 扶南. This gave way to the Zhenla/Gaomian 真腊-高棉 state built around the valley system of the Mekong; it was a more successful kingdom that reached its apogee with a larger Khmer Empire centered around Angkor. Yet even this could not dominate the areas beyond its river system for long and ended up being overrun by tropical jungles.

Further to the west, the Menam river (Chao Phraya) eventually became the heart of dynastic states that the Chinese called *Xianluo* 暹罗 (Siam), whose rulers were related to some of the Southwest Man peoples neighboring Yuan and Ming China. Siam grew to become a strong kingdom but was never secure against enemies from their west where the delta areas of the Salween and the Irrawaddy rivers provided river passages into the interior of modern Burma and where other upland peoples came to establish Theravada Buddhist states. Neverthless, like all the others, none were strong long enough to establish lasting empires.

Thus, at different times, along the southern coasts from the Qiantang river to the Pearl River in China to mainland Southeast Asian polities all the way to today's Myanmar, there had been at least two sets of riverine states. They were separated because the Qin-Han and Tang empires stopped at China's southern coasts. After reaching the sea, the emperors chose to establish their garrisons on land and sea to defend the coastal borders. They seemed to have been content with that once they were clear that there were no threats from maritime enemies. Even the coastal Yue peoples of the south who later became *Tangren* or Tang Chinese did not seek to expand Chinese power. They were content to be skilled maritime folk who could be counted on to venture across the China Seas as imperial sailors when necessary or as merchants whenever they had opportunities to do so.

From ancient times, foreign traders coming to China were always welcome. However, it was a long while before Chinese merchants went forth in their own ships to trade south of the coastal areas. Indeed, it was not until the 10th century that there is evidence of the Chinese venturing beyond the Nanhai to the Indian Ocean to obtain exotic products and build trading links with a large number of Southeast Asian markets. Again it was the Mongol invasion that unleashed China's outreach to its south. Although a continental power, the Mongol Yuan made good use of the navy that the Southern Song had built originally to fight the Khitan Liao and Jurchen Jin forces. Kublai Khan noted that southern Chinese were great sailors and ship-builders. He harnessed their navy to further his imperial adventures.

The southern provinces of Zhejiang, Fujian and Guangdong were where the best ships were built. Their peoples ventured forth to the open seas to fish and trade and, after many centuries, had become fearless sailors who knew how to handle rough seas and typhoons. The Southern Song economy became increasingly dependent on the trade that they brought to China's shores. However, when Kublai Khan took over, he went further. He saw the Song navy as an instrument of power projection and used these Chinese sailors to help him look for other places to conquer. He sent the navy east to attack Japan and south against Vietnam and Champa, even sailing as far south as Java.

In short, 120 years before Zheng He, Kublai Khan had opened China to the south in an aggressive way. As it turned out, his own forays did not lead to very much; he seemed not really to have known what he was doing. On land, however, the Mongols did better when they marched deep southwest into Yunnan and Guizhou, but when they tried to conquer Vietnam, Champa and Myanmar, there again they crossed a bridge too far. As people from the open steppes, they simply could not cope with the jungles of Southeast Asia. Nevertheless, the changes they made did endure. In a matter of decades, the Mongol Yuan had brought the southwest to become an integral part of China's south and thereby outlined the borders between China and Southeast Asia that have remained more or less the same to the present day.

As for the water's edge where imperial rule had stopped, China was open to maritime trade coming from the ports and kingdoms beyond the South China Sea. By the time of Zheng He's naval expeditions, the Chinese had become one of the largest groups trading between China and the Indian Ocean. Such display of naval power did make an impact on the trading patterns of the region after the 15th century. On the other hand, Zheng He concluded that there were no serious enemies that Ming China needed to fear, so the successors of the Yongle emperor stopped the expeditions and left maritime trade mainly to foreign merchants. Officials in Beijing virtually forgot about that navy for the next 400 years. The successor Manchu Qing dynasty was never interested in expanding their economic interests overseas.

It is well known how the Ming dynasty integrated all foreign trade into an elaborate tributary system. They had become conscious that they faced existential threats from the north and formalized a system that enabled their officials to assert direct control of all foreign trade. Together with the *haijin* 海禁 policy, this stopped Chinese merchants from trading overseas while foreigners were allowed to come under tributary conditions. The system was tightly regulated, limiting the trade. However, the enterprising people of Guangdong and Fujian never allowed these rules to get too much in the way. They continued with their private trading even though much of that was decried as "piracy", or as "illegal". Those caught trading without permission were heavily punished.

This was a time when differences in outlook between the southern literati and the merchant and artisan classes became more prominent. The literati who had been denied direct access to the northern sites of wisdom for centuries headed north in larger numbers to the power centre in Beijing to perform their imperial service. Their roles in the court and control of the examinations gave them influence and prestige in the north that they had never previously enjoyed. As a result, they hardly noticed that their compatriots in the south, the trading classes, and even peasants and fishermen, were less impressed. The latter looked further south and saw their wellbeing linked to knowing the South China Sea and the neighboring ports. They greatly valued the freedom to trade abroad and the chance to welcome more foreign merchants to the country.

This dichotomy in outlook differentiated the upper classes that focused on political power in the north from the non-literati who were attracted to wealth-making developments both within and outside the empire. The merchants and artisans were endlessly enterprising, becoming great risk-takers who continually sought opportunities to develop profitable relationships with agencies across the seas. Unfortunately, those reoriented to northern interests did not appreciate their potential for the country's economic development.

The relative indifference of the Ming and Qing elites to the idea that external enemies from the south could be dangerous finally became obvious late in the 19th century. Even after the defeats of the two Opium Wars, the literati supporting the Manchu emperors were confident that the southern borders were manageable. Although aware that the kingdoms and ports beyond the South China Sea had changed hands and stopped sending tribute, most of them still thought that the Anglo-French navies were not an existential threat. Administrators from the north backed by garrison troops would be enough to protect the southern shores.

After the dynastic system was replaced in 1911 and the literati civilization almost totally destroyed, mistakes continued to be made for several decades. Military leaders fought one another to seize power and foreign interests continued to determine what the Chinese contenders for power should do. Among the people, new generations of students in modern schools were liberated to look elsewhere for enlightenment and preferment, notably in the sciences, in commerce and in industrial enterprises, knowledge more in tune with the progress that most Chinese people wanted to attain.

This made the first decades of the 20th century some of the most intellectually alive years in Chinese history. The Chinese seeking modernization wanted to learn everything they could to enable them to make China as strong and prosperous as the imperialist powers. The new national consciousness also sought to revive a sense of pride in Chinese past achievements. Together, this swelled to become something like the "China Dream" that Chinese leaders from Sun Yat-sen down to Xi Jinping were to share, a dream to become as modern as possible without losing the values that made them Chinese.

At the dream's core was the integration of the new Chinese nation as *Zhonghua minzu*, still an ongoing process. One trend was especially prominent. This was the growing influence of enterprising southerners in coastal cities who mastered new business and industrial methods and had different attitudes towards economic opportunities. Most of them had long been in communication with adventurous foreigners and were keenly aware of what China's modern development would require. With the literati out of power, they pushed for new ways to help the country's rejuvenation.

However, these economic leaders were handicapped by being closely associated with foreign enterprises. Patriotic young idealists who objected to those connections chose to support anti-imperialist goals and welcomed the Chinese Communist Party's victory in 1949. Among the new political elites that established the People's Republic, the struggle to redefine the new China led leaders like Mao Zedong to adopt extreme revolutionary goals that included discarding the past and starting afresh to attain a socialist *tianxia*. This reversed much of the earlier modernization efforts and the economy stagnated. The regime thus returned to the traditional position of political and military elites dictating the fate of Chinese lives and forcing the enterprising southerners to their customary peripheral role.

In retrospect, when the People's Republic faced the high tensions of the Cold War, China's eastern and southern coasts became the country's frontline of defence against international enemies. The contest between militant communism and a post-imperial capitalism had triggered hot wars in Korea and Vietnam along China's borders. The challenges of decolonization in Southeast Asia were volatile and China's south once again came into focus, especially when large numbers of the Chinese overseas had to adapt to the nation building struggles in that region.

The new regime chose to turn away from the coasts in the face of the American naval power that supported the Nationalists who had retreated to the island of Taiwan. Mao Zedong sought help overland from the Soviet Union and went so far as to move China's major industrial capacities from the coastal cities into the interior. While this reduced China's vulnerability, it did little to avoid the tensions between the Chinese and their Soviet comrades. Thus, for three decades, continental and security demands had priority and economic growth was severely constrained. Only the exceptional policy towards the British colony of Hong Kong could provide China with some access to the global economy.

Deng Xiaoping's decision to open up the economy, *gaige kaifang* 改革开放, to the outside world was ultimately based on the idea that the modern market economy was primarily maritime. Ever since the 18th century, capitalism was most successful when it utilized the open seas, especially after the Atlantic, Indian and Pacific Oceans were interconnected. This gave the countries of the North Atlantic great advantages. Most of their economic growth came from the industrial and technological inventions that took advantage of the seas to reach out in every direction.

I do not know whether Deng Xiaoping arrived at his reform policies by reflecting on Western successes with this maritime New Global or whether he was simply rejecting the disastrous ambitions of Mao Zedong. Whatever the reasons, Deng Xiaoping's decision was game-changing. By recognizing how much the market economy depended on an open maritime outlook, he enabled China to develop at an astonishing speed since the 1980s. There is no question that his *gaige kaifang* policy was truly a great leap forward and China's southerners with their experience of the open market economy played a vital role in that transformation.

After the Tiananmen tragedy, Deng Xiaoping's southern tour *Nanxun* 南巡 in 1992 was a dramatic climax to his reform programme. It certainly gave a great boost to entrepreneurs everywhere. It was another historical turning point: national reintegration had reached a point when northern Chinese elites joined those in the south to help open up the economy. Some may argue that Deng Xiaoping also opened up the country to problems he did not foresee, for example, the corruption of the Communist Party's senior cadres and the lack of moral compass found among many Chinese people today. Both examples might have been the consequences of opening up quickly at a time when the whole country was in a state of confusion after decades of tight closure. That was unfortunate and probably unavoidable under those circumstances. It certainly does not negate the fact that the transformative changes he inspired have brought great benefits to most of the people of China.

This leads me to one other consequence that deeply affects China's south. For the first time in history, the Chinese have openly proclaimed that they need naval power to protect their widespread economic interests. It is not surprising that China's maritime outreach has become central to its future development. Although political power remains centralized in Beijing, the dynamism of the country's entrepreneurs comes mainly from the kind of openness that southerners have practised for centuries. They are the ones who have long known how to maximize benefits from their outgoing endeavors, including a fine understanding of the need to defend China's maritime interests. They are therefore willing to support the political leadership in the north when their contributions are appreciated.

III. Further South

The changing conditions further south whether at sea or on land clearly require closer attention than ever. Recent events have made clear that the post-war Anglo-American powers saw Southeast Asia as potentially the center of a new strategic zone. As outlined in the preceding chapter, the region has had an extraordinary history. From a number of independent trading kingdoms and autonomous port-cities, they became territories dominated by the West. Nevertheless, their peoples kept pride in their community interests and managed to draw lessons from the periods of subordination. Today, they are engaged in building nation-states with distinct identities, their leaders passionately committed to protect their countries' sovereignty. Although the course of nation building exposed a variety of tensions within and without, the leaders have come together as members of a regional association in order to safeguard their interests against big power rivalries involving countries like the United States, China, India, and Japan.

The region has a complex history of being highly diverse and regularly fragmented into small polities. For them to work together was not normal. During the Vietnam War, it was divided into two parts. The countries fearful of the domino effect by which a communist victory in Vietnam would lead the others to fall under communist control pushed Thailand and four maritime states into the regional Association of Southeast Asian Nations, ASEAN. After the war ended and Vietnam was reunited, ASEAN began to play a useful role for the region by adopting a neutral position between the superpowers.

During the conflict between Vietnam and Cambodia, ASEAN intervened on the side of Cambodia. This led the China that supported Cambodia to reassess its policies and develop a friendly relationship with the Association. By the time the Cold War ended in the 1990s, the conditions were so changed that it became possible for all 10 states of Southeast Asia to set aside their differences. In 1999, all four anti-capitalist states on the mainland agreed to join the six anti-communist original ASEAN states to make the organization fully representative of the region as a whole.

By that time, China was engaged globally with the maritime market economy that effectively connected it with Western Europe and the United States. To everyone's surprise, the Beijing leaders moved quickly to propose an ASEAN-China Free Trade Area and also supported other initiatives to bring ASEAN commercial interests closer to China's own. I mentioned earlier the historic role of the South China Sea that China shares with eight of the Southeast Asian nations. When the rival claims over the reefs and islands in that sea were announced, that attracted the attention of international lawyers and oil companies. Many people thought the differences could be systematically resolved but this was not to be. By the time China became the world's second largest economy and showed its determination to control their claims, its island-building activities led the United States to highlight the freedom of navigation for its naval forces. Together with the ideological differences between the two powers, China's claims have been presented as potential threats to the security and sovereign rights of several ASEAN nations.

China's south is more open than ever but the need to be in control remains strong among the political leaders in Beijing who are sensitive to any threat to their right to rule. I stress this because it helps to explain what is the biggest idea that has come out of China in the past few years. That is the "One Belt One Road" idea or Belt Road Initiative (BRI) that seeks to create more opportunities for future economic growth. However, the key feature of the Initiative is that it is both overland and maritime across areas that had for millennia been the Old World. This makes it a juxtaposition of land and sea strategies by China's leaders and marks their understanding that a balanced approach is essential to advance their long-term interests.

The ancient overland Silk Road and the access to the ports along the ocean highways are the two sides of the vision that demands that China safeguards its national goals when moving in both directions at the same time. Nevertheless, there is a distinction between the overland belt pushing west and north and the maritime road reaching out east and south. The Chinese know their history, so they would expect that the challenges facing each half would be different. The overland Belt across the Eurasian landmass to reach markets in Europe has not been attractive since the end of the Mongol empire. China understands the costs and risks of investing in that route and it is unlikely that Chinese leaders expect its modern manifestation to pay for itself. For example, at the end of the Cold War, China moved to initiate the Shanghai Cooperation Organization (SCO) and offered cooperation and assistance to several Central Asian countries. It was clear that geopolitical advantage and not profits was on everyone's mind: indeed that remains the issue that has induced SCO's neighbors to join the organization.

China's south, however, is a different story. It is now central to future economic development, and keeping the waters secure for China's maritime linkages has never been so important. For the first time in history, the south is an existential problem for its national interests. There are at least three dimensions that are new.

Firstly, China understands that the dynamism in economic globalization depends a great deal on its entrepreneurs and financiers as well as the inventive industrialists who were always better appreciated in China's south. Today Chinese leaders, including those nurtured in the north, strongly support them to devise the best possible methods for the BRI in the south and thus ensure that the economies of all its participants continue to grow.

Secondly, the countries to China's south had never been sovereign states in an overarching international system before. Their new status demands that they be treated with respect and they have organized themselves to protect that status in an uncertain world. This is not to suggest that their association, ASEAN, is now united on all matters of common interest. It is obvious that its members are still struggling to find their way to become more united on several key issues. But the fact that the Association has come this far without any serious breakdown in its interstate relations is remarkable. It is clear that all the states understand how important it is for them to be doing as much as possible together. Insofar as China's leaders understand this, they would need to do everything they can to help them stay together and not allow outside forces to create unnecessary divisions among them.

Thirdly, the South China Sea has become a source of tension between the United States and China. Thus the subject now involves countries not bordering the sea, including US allies like Japan and Australia and some countries of the European Union. The sea has become a focal point in the US reaction to China's rise as a global economic power. It is thus more vital than ever for the region to remain united and confront the harsh realities of that rivalry. Coincidentally, when the Americans redefined their strategic concerns by moving the goalposts from the Asia-Pacific to the Indo-Pacific, that decision has actually made Southeast Asia more central to the competing powers. Where the Chinese are concerned, the waters off their southern coasts have become more than ever the targets of alarmist speculation, an exacerbation of the critical attention that China's communist leaders has been receiving for a long while.

These are new problems in China's south and the Chinese entrepreneurial classes could be expected to have bigger roles to play in the future as China's leaders navigate the challenges ahead. ASEAN also faces changes to its strategic role because of its inter-ocean location; its members will have to learn to respond quickly to the intensified activities that are bound to come. When key leaders of the world met at the ASEAN conference in November 2018, they expanded the range of strategic issues that are now of greater concern to the ASEAN members. No one knows how this region can help resolve the possible threats to peace and prosperity. Regular meetings between ASEAN and its partner states may not be enough if either China or the US insists that ASEAN has sometime in the future to decide which sides it supports.

China does not take the unity of ASEAN for granted. In particular, the Chinese entrepreneurial groups who are determined to advance their interests in the region are aware that China's south is now much more complicated. It is in their interests to ensure that their political leaders in the north fully understand the demands of coastal and maritime outreach. In addition, even among those who already understand the need for close coordination in their work, they also have to contend with related issues arising from the different demands of the economies across ASEAN's land borders. The various BRI proposals to connect China's southwest provinces to the South China Sea and the Bay of Bengal through Vietnam, Laos-Thailand and Myanmar point to the importance of the new dimensions in this broader south. They obviously pose quite different kinds of challenges that need both parts of the Silk Road Initiative to support each other.

Furthermore, there are now millions of settlers of Chinese descent in Southeast Asia who are loyal to their respective nation-states. Most people in south China are able to relate to these communities and know how to deal with them with delicate care. But those responsible among the central elites, especially those of northern origins, have not always found these localized communities easy to understand. If they wish these nationals of Chinese descent to play a positive role in their countries' relations with China, they would have to exercise great sensitivity to their local interests as well as the interests of the countries where they have made their homes.

The final point to make is that ASEAN is now being re-envisaged as a strategic zone for all the powers. This is because the economic dynamism centered in the North Atlantic for the past two centuries is moving to the south-eastern regions of the Old World. That had begun after the end of World War II when economic growth turned westwards across the Americas towards the Pacific. More recently, the main shift has been eastwards from Europe to the Indian Ocean. China's Belt and Road Initiative is thus taking advantage of the new development to extend the long-term benefits to a revived Old World.

Such a decisive move is unlikely to be straightforward as can be seen in the US decision to redefine their key strategic interest in the Indo-Pacific. The Western Pacific and Indian Oceans have always been where all kinds of Old World protagonists were trading for millennia, where the exchange of ideas, cultures and goods had been conducted under conditions of relative peace. Those historical relationships show how that Old World had always been interconnected. A fresh review of that history could help the peoples involved to restore the conditions that had ensured that every part of that larger trading zone had received the benefits accruing to them. The Indo-Pacific as redefined by a hegemonic power on the other side of the Pacific has now become a different kind of strategic zone for the future. This means that, together with the economic shift from the North Atlantic, Southeast Asia as the only region that faces both oceans will become more vital than ever. And this region, although not part of China, is certainly part of China's south.

Bibliography

Publications in English

Alitto, Guy. *The Last Confucian: Liang Shu-ming and the Chinese Dilemma of Modernity.* Berkeley, CA: University of California Press, 1978.

Andrade, Tonio. *Lost Colony: The Untold Story of China's First Great Victory Over the West.* Princeton, N.J.: Princeton University Press, 2011.

Antony, Robert J., ed. *Elusive Pirates, Pervasive Smugglers: Violence and Clandestine Trade in the Greater China Seas.* Hong Kong: Hong Kong University Press, 2010.

Antony, Robert J. and Angela Schottenhammer, eds. *Beyond the Silk Roads: New Discourses on China's Role in East Asian Maritime History.* Wiesbaden: Harrassowitz Verlag, 2017.

Barme, Geremie and Linda Jaivin, eds. *New Ghosts, Old Dreams: Chinese Rebel Voices.* New York: Times Books, 1992.

Bo Zhiyue. *China's Elite Politics: Governance and Democratization.* Singapore: World Scientific, 2010.

Bodde, Derk. *Essays on Chinese Civilization*, edited by Charles Le Blanc and Dorothy Borei. Princeton: Princeton University Press, 1981.

Callahan, William A. and Elena Barabantseva, eds. *China Orders the World: Normative Soft Power and Foreign Policy.* Washington, D.C.: Woodrow Wilson Center Press and Baltimore: Johns Hopkins University Press, 2011.

Chang Hao. *Chinese Intellectuals in Crisis: Search for Order and Meaning (1890–1911).* Berkeley, CA: University of California Press, 1987.

Chesneaux, Jean, ed. *Popular Movements and Secret Societies in China, 1840–1950.* Stanford: Stanford University Press, 1973.

Cheung, Fanny M. and Ying-yi Hong, eds. *Regional Connection under the Belt and Road Initiative: The Prospects for Economic and Financial Cooperation.* London: Routledge, 2018.

Ch'i Hsi-sheng. *Politics of Disillusionment: The Chinese Communist Party under Deng Xiaoping, 1978–1989.* New York: M.E. Sharpe, 1991.

Chow Tse-tsung. *The May Fourth Movement: Intellectual Revolution in Modern China, 1915–1924.* Cambridge, MA.: Harvard University Press, 1960.

Clark, Hugh R. *Community, Trade, and Networks: Southern Fujian Province from the Third to the Thirteenth Century.* Cambridge, UK; New York: Cambridge University Press, 1991.

Cooke, Nola and Li Tana, eds. *Water Frontier: Commerce and the Chinese in the Lower Mekong Region, 1750-1880.* Singapore: Singapore University Press, 2004.

Dikotter, Frank. *The Cultural Revolution: A People's History 1962–1976.* London: Bloomsbury, 2016.

Dirlik, Arif. *Anarchism in the Chinese Revolution.* Berkeley, CA: University of California Press, 1993.

Dirlik, Arif. *Marxism in the Chinese Revolution.* Lanham, Maryland: Rowman & Littlefield Publishers, Inc., 2005.

Eastman, Lloyd E. *The Abortive Revolution: China under Nationalist Rule, 1927–1937.* Cambridge, MA: Harvard University Press, 1974.

Faribank, John K. and Denis Twitchett, eds. *The Cambridge History of China.* Cambridge: Cambridge University Press, 1978–2015.

Fitzgerald, C.P. *The Southern Expansion of the Chinese People: "Southern Fields and Southern Ocean".* London: Australian National University Press, 1972.

Garver, John W. *Protracted Contest: Sino-Indian Rivalry in the Twentieth Century.* Seattle: University of Washington Press, 2001.

Goldman, Merle, Timothy Creek and Carol Lee Hamrin, eds. *China's Intellectuals and the State: In Search of a New Relationship.* Harvard Contemporary China Series, The Council on East Asian Studies. Cambridge, MA.:, Harvard University, 1987.

Guo Xuezhi. *The Ideal Chinese Political Leader: A Historical and Cultural Perspective.* Westport, CT: Praeger Publishers, 2001.

Guo Xuezhi. *China's Security State: Philosophy, Evolution, and Politics.* New York: Cambridge University Press, 2012.

Hamashita, Takeshi. *China, East Asia and the Global Economy: Regional and Historical Perspectives*, edited by Linda Grove and Mark Selden. Abingdon, Oxon; New York, NY: Routledge, 2008.

Hang Xing. *Conflict and Commerce in Maritime East Asia: The Zheng Family and the Shaping of the Modern World, c. 1620-1720.* Cambridge: Cambridge University Press, 2015.

Hsiao Kung-chuan. *A Modern China and a New World: K'ang Yu-wei, Reformer and Utopian, 1858–1927.* Seattle: University of Washington Press, 1975.

Hsu Cho-yun. *Ancient China in Transition: An Analysis of Social Mobility, 722–222 B.C.* Stanford: Stanford University Press, 1965.

Huang Jing. *Factionalism in Chinese Communist Politics.* New York: Cambridge University Press, 2000.

Huang, Philip C. *Civil Justice in China: Representation and Practice in the Qing.* Stanford: Stanford University Press, 1996.

Hung Ho-Fung. *The China Boom: Why China will not Rule the World.* New York: Columbia University Press, 2015.

Ikenberry, G. John, Wang Jisi and Zhu Feng, eds. *America, China, and the Struggle for World Order: Ideas, Traditions, Historical Legacies, and Global Visions.* New York, NY: Palgrave Macmillan, 2015.

Jacques, Martin. *When China Rules the World: The End of the Western World and the Birth of a New Global Order.* New York: Allen Lane, 2009.

Jenner, W.J.F. *The Tyranny of History: The Roots of China's Crisis.* London: Allen Lane, 1992.

Johnson, Chalmers. *Peasant Nationalism and Communist Power.* Stanford: Stanford University Press, 1962.

Kirby, William C., ed. *Realms of Freedom in Modern China.* Stanford: Stanford University Press, 2003.

Lampton, David M. *Following the Leader: Ruling China, from Deng Xiaoping to Xi Jinping.* Berkeley, CA: University of California Press, 2014.

Langlois, Jr., John D., ed. *China under Mongol Rule.* Princeton: Princeton University Press, 1981.

Leibold, James. *Reconfiguring Chinese Nationalism: How the Qing Frontier and its Indigenes Became Chinese.* New York, N.Y.: Palgrave Macmillan, 2007.

Levenson, Joseph R. *Confucian China and its Modern Fate.* 3 vols. Berkeley, CA: University of California Press, 2008.

Li Cheng. *Chinese Politics in the Xi Jinping Era: Reassessing Collective Leadership.* Washington, DC: Brookings Institution Press, 2016.

Li Nan, ed. *Chinese Civil-Military Relations.* New York: Routledge, 2006.

Liang Shuming. *The Philosophy of Eastern and Western Cultures.* The Commercial Press, 1991.

Lieberthal, Kenneth. *Governing China: From Revolution through Reform*, 2nd edition. New York: W.W. Norton & Company, Inc., 2004.

Lieberthal, Kenneth, Cheng Li and Yu Keping, eds. *China's Political Development: Chinese and American Perspectives*. Washington, DC: Brookings Institution Press, 2014.

Lin Yu-sheng. *The Crisis of Chinese Consciousness: Radical Antitraditionalism in the May Fourth Era*. Madison: University of Wisconsin Press, 1978.

MacFarquhar, Roderick. *The Origins of the Cultural Revolution*, 3 vols. New York: Oxford University Press, 1974, 1983, 1997.

MacFarquhar, Roderick and Michael Schoenhals. *Mao's Last Revolution*. Cambridge, MA.: Harvard University Press, 2006.

Moloughney, Brian and Peter Zarrow, eds. *Transforming History: The Making of a Modern Academic Discipline in Twentieth Century China*. Hong Kong: Chinese University Press, 2011.

Muni, S.D. *China's Strategic Engagement with the New ASEAN: An Exploratory Study of China's Post-Cold War Political, Strategic and Economic Relations with Myanmar, Laos, Cambodia and Vietnam*. Singapore: Institute of Defence and Strategic Studies, Nanyang Technological University, 2002.

Narine, Shaun. *Explaining ASEAN: Regionalism in Southeast Asia*. Boulder, CO: Lynne Rienner Publishers, 2002.

Ng Chin-keong. *Boundaries and Beyond: China's Maritime Southeast in Late Imperial Times*. Singapore: NUS Press, 2017.

Ooi Kee Beng. *The Eurasian Core and Its Edges: Dialogues with Wang Gungwu on the History of the World*. Singapore: ISEAS, 2014.

Perdue, Peter C. *China Marches West: The Qing Conquest of Central Eurasia*. Cambridge, MA: Harvard University Press, 2005.

Pieke, Frank N. *The Good Communist: Elite Training and State Building in Today's China*. New York : Cambridge University Press, 2009.

Po, Ronald C. *The Blue Frontier: Maritime Vision and Power in the Qing Empire*. Cambridge, UK: Cambridge University Press, 2018.

Pye, Lucian W. *The Mandarin and the Cadre: China's Political Cultures*. Ann Arbor: Center for Chinese Studies, University of Michigan, 1988.

Schram, Stuart R., ed. *Foundations and Limits of State Power in China*. London: School of Oriental and African Studies, University of London and Hong Kong: Chinese University of Hong Kong Press, 1987.

Schwarcz, Vera. *The Chinese Enlightenment: Intellectuals and the Legacy of the May Fourth Movement of 1919*. Berkeley, CA: University of California Press, 1986.

Schwartz, Benjamin I. *The World of Thought in Ancient China*. Cambridge, MA: The Belknap Press of Harvard University Press, 1985.

Shambaugh, David, ed. *Power Shift: China and Asia's New Dynamics*. Berkeley, CA: University of California Press, 2005.

So, Billy K.L. *Prosperity, Region, and Institutions in Maritime China: The South Fukien Pattern, 946-1368*. Cambridge, Mass.: Harvard University Asia Center, 2000.

Spence, Jonathan D. *The Gate of Heavenly Peace: The Chinese and Their Revolution, 1895–1980*. New York: Viking Press, 1981.

Sukma, Rizal. *Indonesia and China: The Politics of a Troubled Relationship*. New York: Routledge, 1999.

Tang Tsou. *The Cultural Revolution and Post-Mao Reforms: A Historical Perspective*. Chicago: University of Chicago Press, 1986.

Teiwes, Frederick C. *Leadership, Legitimacy and Conflict in China*. Armonk, NY: M.E. Sharpe, 1984.

Teiwes, Frederick C. *Politics and Purges in China: Rectification and the Decline of Party Norms, 1950–1965*. Armonk, NY: M.E. Sharpe, 1993.

Tu Wei-ming, ed. *The Living Tree: The Changing Meaning of Being Chinese Today*. Stanford: Stanford University Press, 1991.

Twitchett, Denis. *The Writing of Official History under the T'ang*. Cambridge: Cambridge Press, 1992.

Unger, Jonathan, ed. *Chinese Nationalism*. New York: M.E. Sharpe, 1996.

Unger, Jonathan, ed. *The Nature of Chinese Politics: From Mao to Jiang*, Armonk, New York: M.E. Sharpe, 2002.

Van Dyke, Paul A. *Merchants of Canton and Macao: Politics and Strategies in Eighteenth-century Chinese Trade*. Hong Kong: Hong Kong University Press, 2011.

Vogel, Ezra F. *Deng Xiaoping and the Transformation of China*. Cambridge, MA: Harvard University Press, 2011.

Wade, Geoff, ed. *China and Southeast Asia*. Six volumes. New York: Routledge, 2008.

Wade, Geoff and James K. Chin, eds. *China and Southeast Asia: Historical Interactions*. London: Routledge, 2018.

Wakeman, Jr., Frederic. *The Great Enterprise: The Manchu Reconstruction of Imperial Order in Seventeenth-Century China*. Berkeley, CA: University of California Press, 1985.

Wang, Edward Q. *Inventing China through History: The May Fourth Approach to Historiography*. Albany, NY: State University of New York Press, 2001.

Wang Gungwu and Ng Chin-keong, eds. *Maritime China in Transition, 1750-1850.* Wiesbaden: Harrassowitz, 2004.

Wang Gungwu. *The Chineseness of China: Selected Essays.* Hong Kong: Oxford University Press, 1991.

Wheaton, Henry. *Elements of International Law: With a Sketch of the History of the Science.* Philadelphia: Carey, Lea & Blanchard, 1836.

White III, Lynn T. *Policies of Chaos: The Organizational Causes of Violence in China's Cultural Revolution.* Princeton: Princeton University Press, 1989.

Wiens, Herold J. *China's March toward the Tropics: A Discussion of the Southward Penetration of China's Culture, Peoples, and Political Control in Relation to the Non-Han-Chinese Peoples of South China and in the Perspective of Historical and Cultural Geography.* Hamden, Conn.: Shoe String Press, 1954.

Womack, Brantly, ed. *Contemporary Chinese Politics in Historical Perspective.* Cambridge: Cambridge University Press, 1991.

Wong, John. *Zhu Rongji and China's Economic Take-off.* London: Imperial College Press, 2016.

Wong, John & Zheng Yongnian, eds. *The Nanxun Legacy and China's Development in the Post-Deng Era.* Singapore: Singapore University Press, 2001.

Wong, John D. *Global Trade in the Nineteenth Century: The House of Houqua and the Canton System.* Cambridge, U.K.: Cambridge University Press, 2016.

Wong Young-tsu, *Search for Modern Nationalism: Zhang Binglin and Revolutionary China, 1869–1936.* Hong Kong: Oxford University Press, 1989.

Wu Yiching. *The Cultural Revolution at the Margins: Chinese Socialism in Crisis.* Cambridge, MA: Harvard University Press, 2014.

Yan Jiaqi and Gao Gao. *Turbulent Decade: A History of the Cultural Revolution.* Translated and edited by D.W.Y. Kwok. Honolulu: University of Hawaii Press, 1996.

Yang Bin. *Between Winds and Clouds: The Making of Yunnan (second century BCE to twentieth century CE).* New York: Columbia University Press, 2009.

Zhao Gang. *The Qing Opening to the Ocean: Chinese Maritime Policies, 1684-1757.* Honolulu: University of Hawaii Press, 2013.

Zhao Litao. *China's Development: Social Investment and Challenges.* Singapore: World Scientific, 2017.

Zheng Yangwen. *China on the Sea: How the Maritime World Shaped Modern China.* Boston: Brill, 2012.

Zheng Yongnian. *The Chinese Communist Party as Organizational Emperor: Culture, Reproduction and Transformation.* New York: Routledge, 2010.

Zheng Yongnian and Lance L.P. Gore, eds. *China Entering the Xi Jinping Era.* New York, NY: Routledge, 2014.

Zheng Yongnian and Huang Yanjie. *Market in State: The Political Economy of Domination in China.* Cambridge, UK: Cambridge University Press, 2018.

Publications in Chinese

包茂红、李一平、薄文泽主编:《东南亚历史文化研究论集》, 厦门: 厦门大学出版社, 2014。

晁中辰著:《明代海禁与海外贸易》, 北京: 人民出版社, 2005。

蔡崇榜著:《宋代修史制度研究》, 台北: 文津出版社, 1991。

陈乔之主编:《面向 21 世纪的东南亚: 改革与发展》, 广州: 暨南大学出版社, 2000。

《邓小平文选》(第一卷) 1938–1965, 北京: 人民出版社, 1989。

《邓小平文选》(第二卷) 1975–1982, 北京: 人民出版社, 1984。

《邓小平文选》(第三卷) 1982–1992, 北京: 人民出版社, 1993。

丁望主编: 《中国文化大革命资料汇编》 (六册), 香港: 明报月刊社, 1967–1972。

高华著:《红太阳是怎样升起的: 延安整风运动的来龙去脉》, 香港:香港中文大学出版社, 2000。

葛兆光著:《宅兹中国: 重建有关"中国"的历史论述》, 北京: 中华书局, 2011。

葛兆光著:《何为中国: 疆域、民族、文化与历史》, 香港: 牛津大学出版社, 2014。

葛兆光著:《历史中國的内与外: 有关"中国"与"周边"概念的再澄清》, 香港: 香港中文大学出版社, 2017。

陈敏之、罗银胜编: 《顾准文集》, 福州: 福建教育出版社, 2010。

顾昕著:《中国启蒙的历史图景: 五四反思与当代中国的意识形态之争》, 香港: 牛津大学出版社, 1992。

贺圣达、王文良、何平著:《战后东南亚历史发展》 1945–1994, 昆明: 云南大学出版社, 1995。

贺圣达、陈明华、马勇、孔建勋著:《世纪之交的东盟与中国》, 昆明: 云南大学出版社, 2001。

胡鞍钢、鄢一龙、魏星著:《2030 中国迈向共同富裕》, 北京: 中国人民大学出版社, 2011。

胡道静主编:《国学大师论国学》, 上海: 东方出版中心, 1998。

李伯重著:《多视角看江南经济史, 1250–1850 》, 北京: 生活·读书·新知
　　三联书店, 2003。

李庆新著:《濒海之地——南海贸易与中外关系研究》, 北京: 中华书
　　局, 2010。

林仁川著:《明末清初私人海上贸易》, 上海: 华东师范大学出版社,
　　1987。

《江泽民文选》共三册: 北京: 人民出版社, 2006.

金灿荣著:《十八大以来中国外交》, 北京: 中国人民大学出版社,
　　2017。

李君如著:《当代中国的马克思主义: 邓小平理论》, 郑州: 河南人民出
　　版社, 1994。

李君如著:《邓小平 —— 当代中国马克思主义的创立者》, 上海: 上海
　　人民出版社, 1995。

李泽厚著:《中国现代思想史论》, 合肥: 安徽文艺出版社, 1994。

梁漱溟著:《东西文化及其哲学》, 陈政, 罗常培编录, 上海: 商务印书
　　馆, 1934 (1922)。

梁漱溟著:《中国文化要义》, 上海: 上海书店, 1989。

刘青峰编:《文化大革命: 史实与研究》, 香港: 香港中文大学出版社,
　　1996。

刘明福著:《中国梦: 后美国时代的大国思维与战略定位》, 北京:中国
　　友谊出版公司, 2010。

《刘少奇选集》(上卷): 北京: 人民出版社, 1981。

《刘少奇选集》(上卷): 北京: 人民出版社, 1985。

《毛泽东文集》(共八册): 北京: 人民出版社, 1993。

潘维主编:《中国模式: 解读人民共和国的 60 年》, 北京: 中央编译出
　　版社, 2009。

乔治忠著:《中国官方史学与私家史学》, 北京: 北京图书馆出版社,
　　2008。

钱穆著:《中国历代政治得失》, 香港: 新华出版社, 1956。

钱穆著:《从中国历史来看中国民族及其中国文化》, 香港: 香港中文大
　　学出版社, 1979。

瞿林东著:《唐代史学论稿》增订本, 北京: 高等教育出版社, 2015。

瞿林东著:《中国史学的理论遗产》, 北京: 北京师范大学出版社, 2005。

时殷弘著:《全球性挑战与中国: 多事之秋与中国的战略需要》, 长沙:
　　湖南人民出版社, 2010。

宋永毅主编:《文化大革命: 历史真相和集体记忆》, 香港: 田园书屋,
　　2007。

吴敬琏著:《当代中国经济改革教程》,上海: 上海远东出版社, 2010。

吴敬琏著:《吴敬琏自选集》,北京: 学习出版社, 2009。

许倬云著:《我者与他者: 中国历史上的内外分际》,香港: 中文大学出版社, 2009。

许倬云著:《说中国: 一个不断变化的复杂共同体》,桂林: 广西师范大学出版社, 2015。

陈永发、沈怀玉、潘光哲(访问许倬云),周维朋(记录)著:《家事、国事、天下事: 许倬云八十回顾》,香港: 中文大學出版社, 2011。

《习近平谈治国理政》(两册): 北京: 外文出版社, 2014。

相蓝欣著:《2025 中国梦: 中国不是"崛起"而是"东山再起"》,长沙: 湖南人民出版社, 2010。

熊景明、宋永毅、余国良主编:《中外学者谈文革》,香港: 香港中文大学当代中国文化研究中心, 2018。

严家其著:《"文化大革命" 十年史》,香港: 万年青图书中心, 1989。

杨国桢著:《闽在海中: 追寻福建海洋发展史》,南昌: 江西高校出版社, 1998。

阎学通著:《中国国家利益分析》,天津: 人民出版社, 1996。

阎学通等编:《中国与周边中等国家关系》,北京: 社会科学文献出版社, 2015。

余英时著:《现代儒学论》,新加坡: 八方文化创作室, 1996。

余英时著:《犹记风吹水上麟: 钱穆与现代中国学术》,台北: 三民书局, 2015。

俞新天著:《探索中国与世界的互动: 现代化、地区合作与对外战略》,上海: 上海人民出版社, 2012。

赵汀阳著:《天下体系: 世界制度哲学导论》,北京: 中国人民大学出版社, 2011。

郑必坚著:《关于历史机遇和中国特色社会主义的战略道路》,上海:上海人民出版社, 2005。

郑筱筠主编:《东南亚宗教与社会发展研究》,北京: 中国社会科学出版社, 2013。

INDEX

.

Printed in the United States
By Bookmasters